Samuel Riggins' Letter collection of the First World War

"Write Real Soon"

Denton, Texas 76203

Published Independently by Rainbow Crow Publishing

Sam Riggins, Liberty, South Carolina – First World War

Introduction

This collection of 101 letters written by Sam Riggins, a young man from Liberty, South Carolina to his future wife, Arabella Smith, is a wonderful example of blossoming love during war.[i] Both grew up in the small town of Liberty, South Carolina before its Textile Era (1900-1980). Sam's christened name was Samuel Leonard Riggins, born October 4, 1875, and his death was recorded on April 13, 1974. Arabella "Arrie" Smith was born in 1897 and she passed away in 1948. Sam then married Catherine Janice Ponder in 1949 who was a schoolteacher.[ii]

Liberty, South Carolina, the town Sam and Arabella lived in was incorporated March 2, 1876, and members of the town changed the name from Liberty Springs to Liberty. The town was included in the Pendleton District, which in our contemporary era consist of the counties of Anderson, Oconee, and Pickens. During the Antebellum Period (pre-Civil War), most of the members of the community were subsistence farmers and did not own slaves. After the Civil War, Union soldiers remained in the area until 1868 and Reconstruction divided the Pendleton District into Pickens and Oconee Counties.[iii] The Charlotte-Atlanta Airline Railway made Liberty a stopping point on its route.

Liberty did not receive its post office until 1873 and after 1901 became a booming textile community with the first cotton mill in the area.

Sam was stationed in the Military Branch around Chattanooga, Tennessee and trained in Camp Wadsworth in Spartanburg, South Carolina, before making his way towards deployment to France as a Sergeant. He remained in Company "C" of the 16th Machine Gun Battalion and was a part of the 6th Infantry which earned the nickname "The Sightseeing 6th Infantry Division."

November 10, 1917
Miss Arrie Smith,
My dearest friend,

I am just like you, have not answered anybody's letters yet, am going to answer yours, if nobody else get an answer.

I am real well and hope that you are the same I would have answered but have been awfully busy.

You said that you would tell me what Winnie-Sue said when I came home xmas, may not get to come if I do you will get a chance, because I am certainly coming over there next time I get home.

I go visiting most every Sunday. We boys get together and crack walnuts and hickory nuts for pass time it is pretty lonesome sometimes up here, so you see, we have to do something to keep off the blues. Just a word from you will assist in keeping them off, any time, it you have not got time to write much I will appreciate a short letter but had rather have a long one.

Please write soon, Your true friend, Cpl. Sam Riggins.

Give my best regard to Mr. Smith and excuse this hastily written letter.

December 17, 1917
2:00 am
I will answer you letter just as soon as possible, no passes are to be issued, so won't get to come Xmas.

Sam

[P.S.] The weather is two below zero

December 29, 1917
My dearest friend,

Your present, which, you sent to me was certainly appreciated. Thank you very much. I am real well but am still quarantined. I got a three day pass and went home, sure did want to see you but did not have time to go anywhere hardly. My father got hurt and sent me a telegram, if he had not wouldn't have gotten any pass. It took me one day to go home and one to come back, so , you see that I had no time to see anybody. It does seem to me that we out to have the privilege of visiting our friends sometime.

Did you enjoy the Xmas holidays? I enjoyed them very well but did not enjoy them as much as would have if I had not been in the army. (Some time I hope to spend Xmas with you.) If it wasn't for the hopes I have, don't know what I would do if my trip home was to be gone over I would stay over time and come to see you but that is a pretty serious thing to do. I always wanted to obey orders but, thought very seriously of staying over what my pass allowed and coming to see you, then I knew that you had rather forgive one boy not coming than to have one disobey orders. You remember that I wrote and told you that, was sure coming to see you but I could not. I heard from Henry Howard last week, he is attending Firman [sic], am proud of him. I think that he is one of the best boys that I've ever met with.

Wishing you a happy new year, I am as ever, Your truest friend, Cpl. Sam Riggins. (Please answer real soon to the boy that loves you most, Sam)

January 14, 1918
Dear Arrie,

My mind is centered upon marrying this afternoon. I suppose it is because Queen Johann got married. When girls and boys of her age gets to marrying, I think that it is time for me to consider, don't you? Her marriage sure was a surprise to me, it looks as though every young person in that community is going to marry.

Are your enjoying this cold weather? I am not, the thermometer registered twenty-two below zero this morning but I can not think that it was that cold although, it is colder here than it ever was down at Liberty.

Arrie, I sure have got the blues, don't know why. Did you ever have them? I know that you never had them as bad as I have got them now. I do not know what to do with myself, have tried to content myself in every way imaginable but everything has lost its enjoyment so far as I am concerned at present. With kindest regards and best wishes, I remain,

Your sincere friend, Cpl. Sam Riggins

P.S. Please answer real soon.

January 24, 1918
Dearest Friend,

This [day finds me] real well and hope that it will find you the same. The blues is not worrying me so much tonight, got many letters today. When I get lots of mail I do not have the blues so if you want to keep a soldier boy from having the blues, why just write to me real often. I don't know why, but a letter from you is appreciated more than one from any other person, wish that I could get one from you every day but I know that you do not have time to write that often.

You did not tell me who that was that visited you, would like to know. I sure do wish that I could have been there. It would have been pleasure enough for me if I had not seen anyone except you.

I have got recus [sic] turned to the cold weather and do not get very cold. At first I thought I never could get used to it but, don't care now if the weather is cold. The ground is still covered with snow and has been almost all winter. We have loaf bread exclusively to eat. I have not ate any biscuit bread since I left home Christmas, except a little treat my sister sent to me.[iv] Any kind tastes all o.k. to me, don't care what kind. I weigh one hundred and seventy pounds, the most that I have every weighed, have gained forty pounds since I enlisted. So, you can see that we get a good deal to eat and that is what I want, don't care anything about how much I drill if I can get lots to eat and plenty of mail.

Since I have been transferred, don't think that I will go to France any time soon, probably a year from now. A machine your man is supposed to know a good deal before he goes over there. Our Lieutenants say that it is the highest branch of service but I had rather think that the Aviation Corp is the highest branch.[v] I will close by asking you to write to me real soon.

Your friend, Sam Riggins

February 8, 1918
Dearest friend,

I have been wondering why you have not answered my letter. You know that your letters are always rec'd gladly, that is when you write them to me. I don't want to worry you about writing to me but would be very glad to have you write to me sometimes. I will answer all letters that I receive from you.

Arrie, do you see Henry Howard very often? I don't know of any boy that I think more of than I do him. I wish that we had lots of boys of his type, don't you? I rec'd a letter from Prof. Givens and he told me that Henry was attending school at Firman [sic].[vi] No doubt he will make good.

I am on guard to night but I don't care because the company is but having night maneuvers. I just as soon do guard as to get out and ramble all night. I don't like the idea of drilling at nights very much.

I will ask you to pardon me for writing to you when you do not write to me and will also ask you to answer real soon. Your sincere friend, Sam Riggins

February 13, 1918
Dear Arrie,

Your excuses were excepted, don't blame you for not writing when you so much work to do but you know that, would be glad to hear from you, even when you do not have time to write, so you may easily see I want you to write every time that your time permits. You said that one of your reasons for not writing to me was that I mentioned about getting four letters on the same day that, rec'd yours. Well, they were from my brothers, excepting one, which, was from Prof. Givens. I don't get very much mail but, would be glad to get lots of it from you.

I hope that you won't be drafted and, know that you won't, although, in Europe there are several Regiments of women, hope that America will never have to depend upon the women to do the fighting.[vii] I know that they can fight alright but they are, badly, out of their places, when they do, don't you think so?

I, for one, could appreciate an honorable peace but, think that it will be sometime before we get it, aren't your of the same opinion? No, most people could appreciate peace better in a year from now. I think by the time it comes that they will be prepared to appreciate it.

No, Arrie, I have not learned how to dance, perhaps, you would be surprised if you knew that I have not been with but one girl since I enlisted and that was while I was at home the first time.[viii]

I must stop and let one of the Y workers use the typewriter.[ix] Please, answer real soon, with a long letter.

Your truest friend, Cpl. Sam Riggins

P.S. You said that you hoped to write a more interesting letter next time that you wrote to me, don't think that you could write a more interesting one, than the last one and I know that there isn't another person that could write one near so interesting to me.

February 21, 1918
Dearest Friend,

Have just rec'd your letter, and answering it, now so that you may get the answer before Sunday. If you don't get the answer by then, I won't get to hear from you until week after next, don't want to wait that long to hear from you.

I did not go to Sunday school last Sunday but do go very often. I attend a great many religious services during the week. Most every night one may attend services at one of the several Ys, which we are fortunate to have near our camp. The different churches of Chattanooga hold most of these services.[x] I do not know how the boys will do after they get into France but, don't think that the influence of the Christian people of Chattanooga can ever die. I try, each day to become a better boy and am going to strive to abstain the things which are worth while, so that when I return, will probably be of some use, in the uplift of the better things of life.

I still try to sing but you know that we [boys] not have the opportunity of singing very much, when he's in the army. I have learned the habit of trying to sing even when out on the hikes. All of my associates say that, am always happy but they do not always know.

I know that you are doing your part in the war, that we are involved in but I think that you should rest sometimes. The people whom we are depending on to win this war is the people that are producing the food, don't you think I'm right? The reason that I think you should rest sometimes, we rest very often and I think that the farm people should rest so much as we.

I think that your father has got a profitable job, that is, if he takes all of the [hullabaloo] which the people are not allowed to have. I suppose that they have an allowance do they not? I know that they do up here. I hope that he will like his job fine.

I am in quarters, had have no ink except this red, which the supply Sgt composed for the purpose of marking clothing but I know that you will pardon me for using it, won't you? I did not ans. All the questions that you asked in your last letter, was in a hurry you see, we must be always be on tie in everything so in order to be there I very often have to omit things which, would enjoy writing to you if you will pardon me, will try to ans [sic] all from now on. I sure will be glad to see spring come, have been out in so much cold during this winter. But want to be satisfied even when the most ideal weather comes.

I am not very rand of having, myself, but think that would enjoy helping you then cotton this spring. All that would worry me, you would not enjoy my helping you, that is if you were compelled to listen to my long tongue.

Our company commander said that we would never go over the top, we are to be back in rear of the front lines trenches and our guns are to form a barrage fire, that very satisfactorily for me. Awaiting the pleasure of your earliest reply, I am as ever

Your sincere friend, Sam Riggins

March 4, 1918
Sunday 6 pm

Dearest friend,

I went on guard duty yesterday afternoon at five o'clock and have just been relieved. Am real well and hope that you are the same.

I get homesick just as bad as ever, no difference that I can tell. I can't forget some folks, although no one up here knows that I get homesick. I keep all of that to myself except what I tell you. I do not think that I'll be able to get a pass during this summer, however, I am going to try for one, regardless of doubts.

Dwight is out of the hospital for the first time in several weeks. He has had pneumonia and eye troubles, hope that he won't have to go to the hospital again.

I spent the twenty second of February playing baseball and singing. Did I tell you about meeting Mr. McGlowery. He composed the song entitled "Onward Mighty Army," and several other songs that you find I used to sing. Wish that you could hear him sing. He's now a member of the Fifty Third Infantry. I hate to see a man like him in the army. It does not make any difference about such fellows as myself that can't do much for the community, in which they lived, if they were to go back there but I would like to see such men as he, go back and do a greater work than they can do in the army.

I will ask you to excuse this letter. Everything seems like a dream to me just now no wonder. I did not go to bed last night at all.

I had all of my teeth fixed during the past week, that were decayed. Am still nervous you know how one feels about teeth, don't you? Hoping to get that page of questions, real soon. I remain, as ever,

Your Sincere friend, Sam Riggins.

March 7, 1918
Dearest friend,

Your letter just Recd, and was appreciated very much. I am real well and truly hope that you are the same.

I started a little souvenir to you, if is not of any use but I thought that it was real pretty, hope that you will get it all O.K. It is my first one to send to any girl. I do not understand myself, it seems impossible for me to think of any girl except you. For awhile, when I'd think of you, I would say to myself that I was not going to think of you all of the time when, not drilling and, would go to the Y, and try to forget all about you but I found it impossible. The reason that, didn't want to think of you was that I knew that you cared nothing for me and did not want me to think of you. Pardon me for writing this paragraph. I knew that you will not appreciate it and am not going to express my feelings to you.

I hope that you won't have to walk to school any more because I know how hard it is to walk, have to walk sometimes, myself. Maybe it will rain real often so Mr. Smith can't plow.

I have got to go out and drill two hours tonight. I do not know what kind of drill it is going to be but hope that it won't be very hard. I do not like the idea of drilling at nights, think that we can do enough during the days, don't you think so too?

You said that it would have been hard for you to stayed awake for twenty four hours and that you would have been likely to a slept on your post. If anyone should go to sleep while on post he would be put in the Guard House but fortunately, for me and all other Corporals we never have to walk any post, are in charge of a Relief I could have slept but, would have gotten my Blankets dirty on the floor because that was all the place that there were to spread them so, rather than have dirty Blankets, would stay awake. I must step and stand Retreat, so, answer real soon to your

Own true and affectionate friend, Corp Sam Riggins

March 15, 1918

Dearest Friend,

As usual, I was glad to get your letter. I am real well and hope that you are the same.

I am not drilling because today is a holiday for us Soldiers in Co. C and you know that I am enjoying myself. I have not drilled very much in sometime, have been going to school most the time. I enlisted to shoot and not to go to school but, have come to the conclusion that they are going to send me to school most of the time. I never liked to go to school but, don't like to drill so, I am not making any complaints.

One of our Lieutenants left for France last week, suppose that we will go before very long. I thought for awhile that we would not go before July or August but guess that we will. The Lieutenant that went to France will join us when we get there. Most every letter that I get from some is one that ask if I don't think that the war will stop pretty soon. I don't know how to answer such a question but they need not look for peace yet. Anyone may see that this war is not going to stop for a long time. Or that is my opinion about it, what is yours? I am not worrying a great deal but suspect that I will before I am through with the army.

Papa said that he was coming to see me sometime about the fifth Sunday in this month. I will certainly be glad to see him. I know how to appreciate homefolks and friends now.

I can't hardly write on account of a big Band that is playing right in my ears. I like to hear music but, would be glad if it would stop long enough for me to finish this letter.

It looks as though I will be able to get a pass before I go to France, am trying my best to get one. If I do, am coming to see you regardless of every other friend that I have, providing that you have no objections.

Answer real soon to your, Sincere friend, Sam

March 20, 1918
Dear Arrie,

After receiving your letter today, I went to get some pictures that I had took last week, was aiming to send one to you but the photographer had lost them. He said that he wanted to try to find them so, I probably will get them in time to send one out next week. If don't, will go to Chattanooga and have some made especially for you. I sure do want one of yours. I thought that you had forgotten about me wanting one but am sure glad that you haven't.

I attended Church last Sunday away but in the country. I mean away from camp. One of my friends and I went out or a walk and after walking for sometime we found the Church which I attended. They had the new Vaughan books. I tried to play the organ but couldn't play those new songs very well. They invited me back so think that I will go in next Saturday evening. They are going to practice some special songs for Easter. I'm going to try to help them but can't do very much.

I do hope that you will succeed in getting a new school building. That one, which you spoke of is pretty small for school, especially Sunday School. Suppose everybody attends S.S. do they not?

You said that you pretty near always meant what you said. That is one of the many things that I admire about you. I can always depend upon what you tell me. I admire a girl that does not try to flatter me, as that is what I call it.

The lights are going out and I want this to leave tonight so must stop. Will write more next time. With kindest regards and best wishes, I remain as ever, Your sincere friend, Sam Riggins. Answer real soon

March 28, 1918
Dearest friend,

Am going to start this letter by answering the questions which I ought to have answered in my last letter to you.

I am not sure about your age but think that you were twenty on your last birthday. Am I [right] or wrong? I will be twenty-two years young on the twenty sixth day of April. Perhaps I should not tell my age because that sounds old even though I am younger than ever or at least I feel that way.

I, tho, wonder who will marry next. Just rec'd a letter from Papa stating that Mary Henderson and Frank Kirby was married on last Sunday. It does look like my time would come doesn't it? (But you are the only girl that I am particular about writing to so, don't guess that my time will ever come. You will be the judge of that.) Papa also stated in his letter that Henry and himself would arrive in Chattanooga on next Sunday morning, don't suspect that I will try to sing any Easter songs. Am going to meet them at the Depot, if I possibly can.

Beginning tonight, I am going to take type writing so long as I'm in the [Chickamauga] Park.[xi] Will practice at least one hour each day, and as much over as time permits.

Yes, I keep up with the war news, read two papers each day. A morning and an evening, both published in Chattanooga. I am not worrying over the war very much but, do think that prayer would assist more than anything else in the struggle which we are involved in.

If I should start to France now it would be, probably, two months before I arrived there. I read a letter the other day from one of my friends that left here three months ago and he's in England now. It takes a long time to transport troops across as this is what he say about it.

It might be a long time before I received your letter, if you were to write one and I were to leave before I got it, but it would finally come to me so you need not worry about me getting it. Answer real soon, Your sincere friend, Sam

April 1, 1918
Dear Arrie;

Will write you a few lines to let you know that I'm still in Chickamauga Park and am real well, hope that you are well too.

I am not considering this an answer to the letter, which, I received from you yesterday, will answer it just as soon as I arrive at the place where I am going.

I will keep absolutely, clean, if I did not consider you worth living for, would not tell you that I thought anything of you at all but I do consider you worth living for and will tell you that I think more of you than anything in this world, am not telling you this merely to have something to write but, mean every word that I am saying. When I return and the War is over, am going to offer to you a body that has been protected in every way that I could protect it.[xii]

You need not answer this, will write to you again as soon as I arrive at the place where I am to go.

Yours, Sam

P.S. Possibly, you think that I am saying more than I should about the way that I intend to conduct myself but I want you to know just where I stand. I put Character above everything else. I want you to consider my life before you ever say the words that I did. I said that I was going to depend upon you to be my wife and I sure did consider before saying those words. Of course, you could not say that you were expecting me to be your wife but you could say that you were expecting me to be your husband. I had rather hear that than anything that I know of but don't want you to say it unless you judge me to be a real man.

S.R.

April 14, 1918
Dear Arrie;

In order to make good my promise, I went to Chattanooga and had those pictures taken yesterday, will send one to you just as soon as I get them, am going to expect one of yours, in return.

I attended a Social at Chattanooga yesterday, the first thing of its kind that I have attended since I enlisted, enjoyed it very well. The Pastor of the First Christian Church delivered a speech, in behalf of the Soldiers, which, I enjoyed immensely. He said that the only fault that he had found of us, we were to independent. He, also, said that the people of Chattanooga wanted to be used by the Soldiers and he hoped that we would use them more in the future than we had in the past.

I am not taking Typewriting for the purpose of getting a position, don't want one. I was offered a position as Company Clerk but refused it, had rather do my bit in the ranks. I can't write with a pen and that is the reason that I'm taking a course in Typewriting.

I won't promise to kill any Germans but will promise to use every ounce of energy that I have trying to do so.

No, I have not studied any of the lessons that has been published in the Trench and Camp.[xiii] I did not even know that there had been any published. I have gotten into the habit of glancing over the papers and just picking out the articles that interest me and letting the balance go unread. That is a bad habit for one to get into, isn't it?

The Officers are transferring a lot of the boys out of our Company because they are not fit to be in it or at least the Officers says they are not. It takes a lot of energy to be of any use in a Machine Gun Battalion.[xiv]

No one likes to eat better than I but you would not make me homesick by mentioning Strawberries and Cream. (I do get homesick when I think of you and that is pretty near all of the time.) I can stand to be hungry better than I can being away from my friends.

Your letter has just arrived, was mailed the fourth of April or rather written then. I had almost give up in despair when it came.

I notice all kinds of mistakes in the above but, have not got to rewrite it so please excuse me for making them and I will try to not make so many next time.

With kindest regards and best wishes, I remain as ever, your truest friend, Sam. Please, answer real soon.

April 26, 1918
Dear Arrie;

Have just arrived at this place and, suspect that I am the sleepiest fellow that has ever arrived here, however, I am going to write you a few lines and let you know that I am real well. I hope that this will find you feeling well too.

I was expecting to send you a picture of myself but they have not come yet, don't know why. I suppose that they will come pretty soon if they don't, will have some more made. I am determined for you to get one.

The members of my Co. are packed up and are ready to leave for I don't know where. The boys all think that we are going to Spartanburg, S.C. hope that we do, can see you sometimes then.[xv]

I am going to depend upon those last words that you told me or rather, am going to depend upon you to be my friend and after the War is over I am going to depend upon you to be my wife and if you don't do it I will never have a wife. I am putting all of my trust in you. I have never talked like this to any other girl because I never loved any other girl only as a friend. I know that this letter will not be interesting to you but I just want you to know that I am depending upon you and you alone. I will try not to write any love after this letter. You spoke about how you wanted me to live, you may rest assured that I will live a Clean life, one that will make me worthy of you so far as that is concerned.

Arrie the Co. Commander has sent for me to come and draw the rest of my equipment. So will have to go. Your truest friend, Sam. Answer real soon and excuse this letter.

April 27, 1918
Dearest friend;

Am sending that picture at last, it is not a good one, however it is very much like the original, hope to get the one that you promised me real soon.

We will leave here not later than Tuesday or that is what the Officers say. I don't know where we will go but just remember that I'm thinking of you and am living for you, and sometime I will come back to you. If I thought that, wouldn't I never would have told you what I did in the last letter that I wrote. You may think that I never considered before saying what I did but I sure did think, would not tell a girl that I was depending upon her without thinking along time and that is exactly what I did.

I went down and saw Winnie-Lee before starting back but did not have long to stay because the Train ran to quick. She told me several good things about you but I already knew all of them. I tried to get her to tell me what she told you but she would not.

You have a letter from me already and I know that you won't have time to read so much so, will stop for now. Good night, Your truest friend, Sam. Write soon

May 6, 1918
Dear Arrie,

Have not got the time to write much but will write all that I can. Am real well and hope that you are the same.

I thought that we might have gone to France but instead of that we came to Camp Wadsworth, don't know how I am going to like it but hope that will like fine. We won't be here very long as at least. I don't think that we will, hope to see you before I go away and if, don't it want be my fault.

I must stop for now. Can't write any more just now. Write real soon,
Yours, Sam Riggins

May 12, 1918
Dear Arrie,

I'm sorry that you'll have to read this or try to read this pencil marking but, am on duty and can't do any better. I received both of your letters Friday and answered them that night but did not mail the answers because, was expecting to visit you today. I do not know that will get to visit you while I am here. My job is drilling recruits drafted … and I won't have the opportunity of visiting anyone much.

I can't attend S.S. today, will have to drill recruits all day but will try to be good just the same. It is going to be hard for me to be good because I am tired, worked last night until about ten o'clock putting up tents. I may ball out some of these drafted fellows but won't if I can help it.

You will be writing a great deal of your time if you write as often as I answer your letters.

I arrived here on the same day that I wrote you that letter, did not have time to write very much but did the best that I could. I have stopped writing to all girls except you and Winnie Lee and am going to stop writing to her. Remember, that I am not asking you to stop writing to other boys, don't want you too. I want you to have all the pleasure that you can and if it was any pleasure for me, I would write to other girls but you are the girl and the only girl that I can write to and enjoy myself while doing it. You may neither love me but you may rest assured that you have all of my love. I do not ask you to love me that's up to you.

I must stop and eat breakfast. Always, Sam

Answer real soon. My address is the same, although I'm drilling men in the 16th Co. and am staying in the 16th. The object of my drilling them is to pick out the men that think would suit us best in the M.G. Bat. [Machine Gun Battalion]

May 15, 1918
Dear Arrie,

I have not got many letters to write, therefore can answer yours just as soon as it arrives. I am real well and, hope that you are the same.

No, I do not like to tell these men over here that they must do things but, suspect that they think I do.

I do not want you to get sleepy when writing to me, if it make your letters shorter. Want long letters and lots of them, from you.

I wanted to tell you that [I] was aiming to get a pass and visit you Sat. but you might expected me over and I might not get to come, therefore, will not tell you anything about it, do not know that, can get a pass. You see, I'm trying to avoid disappointments. I think that the [company] runs several trains on Sun.

I have just received a truck and camp from Chickamauga Park, was almost like a letter from home, you see, I felt at home when up there. I do not like this place at all but there's no use of complaining about it.

I am in a tent but away from the Y. and just have two sheets of paper so, will mark all over these two sheets, and when I have plenty of paper again, may do the same thing only I will mark on more than two sheets, that is if, you do not mind me writing on both sides of the paper. Of course, you see I am just obeying the orders given at the bottom of the sheets.

You have the same opinion that my sister has. She balls me out every time that she writes because I do not write more. I have time now to write long letters but do not think that you would appreciate any more than I write. If you want longer letters, just say so in your next letter and you shall have them.

I am going to try to get Mr. McGeaury [sic] to go home with me before one and sing at Smith's grave but do not know that he can go because he's a Co. Clerk now and can't get off from duty very often.

Arrie, do not blame me for telling you that I loved you, it's not my fault. I tried to keep from it but it is hard for me to love a person and not tell them about it. I am really ashamed of myself because I always thought that I had control of myself but, will have to adjust that you control me now. Of course, it you had told me a lot of thing that were untrue you would not have, but you always tell the truth.

Yours, Sam Riggins, Answer soon.

May 21, 1918
Dear Arrie,

I suspect that you are wishing that all of the men were across on the other side of the North Sea. I believe that is the place where you very [well] want them to be, is it not?

I arrived here at 12 o'clock just as my pass expired, so did not have to go to the Mill. I sure did enjoy myself yesterday, am looking forward to the day when I will see you again, hope that it won't be long.

With kindest regards and best wishes, I remain as ever,

Yours, Sam, P.S. Answer real soon.

May 25, 1918
Dear Arrie,

Am answering your letter by return mail so, you can't say that I do not write when I should. Am real well and, hope that you are the same.

I wrote you a few lines on last Monday but guess that they had not reached you when you wrote the letter, which, I received last night. I hope that you have received them by now because I want you to get every line that I write.

I heard Miss Wilson sing at Y. #99 on last Tuesday night.[xvi] She's a real good singer or that is my opinion of her. She said several good things about the regular army but said nothing about the others. Suspect that helped me to enjoy her singing, so not you?

I enjoyed reading the story "The Measure of A Man" and, thought that it was real good. I read it over three times so you may have an idea that I enjoyed it.

I am back with my Co. now but still my job is drilling recruits, like it better than I did at first. I will have to go to the Target Ranges on next Tuesday and stay there for some time. If you can possibly answer this in time for me to get it before that time, I will appreciate it very much. If you can't I will appreciate your answer when it does come.

I won't have any one else express their opinions of your letters. I will risk my own judgment at all times. I will not get offended much I know that you want to make me so, therefore you need not worry about offending me. Anything that you want to write just write it at any time and do not be afraid of making me angry at you. I hope that you will just remember that I won't get angry until you want me to.

I am in my tent and have not suitable place in which to write but, hope that you can read enough of this letter to understand the things that I mean. I doubt if I could read it myself, even though, it is my marking.

I, too, hope that nothing will ever occur that will keep you from trusting me. I am going to expect you to believe the things that you know about me instead of believing the things that you may hear about me. You see, I never even thought of saying that I did not know whether I would answer your letter or not but at that time you gave me credit for saying it. I know that you will not believe those kind of things again.

If my writing will prevent your frowning I will see that you do not have to frown very much while I'm at this place, when I get in France it will be different but, will write as often as I can. I do not want you to wait for answer from your letters then but write as often as you can. I will appreciate every letter that you write to me.

I am as ever, yours, Sam, Answer real soon

May 30, 1918
Dear Arrie,

I want you to know that I appreciated your picture which I read on last Sunday. I was real glad to get it, think that it is a real good picture of you. If there's any chance, am going to carry it to France with me, not that I can't remember how you look but I want it to look at when I'm off of duty, over there. I was, also, real glad to get your letter, it reached me about an hour ago. I would have written you on my way up here but did not have the opportunity, was three days hiking up here and you may know that I'm not rested very much. Arrived here at twelve o'clock today and put up tents this afternoon. I feel much better than I did before your letter came, do not think that it could have reached me in a better time.

Several of our recruits fell out on the way up here but I think that they have all been recounted for so, won't have to worry about them tonight. It kept me pretty busy looking after their packs and other equipment on the marches. I have been arguing that we fellows that have been in service for a year could not stand any more hiking than any body else but, won't argue that way many more. None of the old fellows fell out. With kindest regards and best wishes I remain as ever,

Yours, Sam Riggins, Answer real soon

P.S. I will write to you again real soon so, do not think that I am not writing enough. I have not written but three letters since I left Chattanooga except what I wrote to you, do not write very much. Write a long letter, please.

June 6, 1918
Dear Arrie,

I do not want to send to you an envelope full of excuses but I want you to know that I have had no time to write since writing you last.

I would have enjoyed nothing better than helping you pick those beans, you asked me to help you pick but you know that I have a boss and can't do the things that I enjoy.

I attended a N.Y. School on last Sunday. I have had only one Sunday off in about six weeks and, was with you on that Sunday. I would certainly enjoy visiting you before I go over but I can't do so. I am sure that we will not be here very long. I enjoyed every line that you wrote. You need not worry about me not enjoying your letters.

I have just a few things that I want you to keep in mind and, will tell you one of them, at least. I want you to know that I will keep you in my mind until I return to you and, will keep all of my trust in you until then. I won't have the opportunity of writing to you when I want from now on but I want you to write to me as often as you can. Every line that you write to me will help to make me a real soldier. I mean a Christian Soldier.

Answer real soon, Yours, Sgt. Sam Riggins

Excuse hastily markings and if I am off on next Sunday, will write to you a long letter.

June 6, 1918
Dear Arrie,

I wrote a letter to you today after noon, but am going to take advantage of a few spare moments and write another one.

I am real well and, hope that you are the same. I, also, hope that Mr. Smith is well again.

You give Mr. and Mrs. Sherieff [sic] my congratulations when you give them yours, will you? I truly hope that they will have a long and happy life. I have already told you enough for you to know that I am going to continue to love you always, therefore, will not tell you anything more about it unless you want me to. As, I told you before, I will never have a wife unless I get you. So, I'm going to leave it all up to you.

I want you to tell me in your next letter whether or not you love me. I think that you ought to know by this time. I am going to expect you to tell me.

I know that you understand that I have no place in which to write. So, it isn't necessary for me to ask you to excuse sorry markings. Those men who fell out on the hike from Wadsworth here are all o.k. now.

Answer real soon. Yours, Sgt. Sam Riggins

P.S. I am sending you a book of the songs that we sing.

June 8, 1918

Dear Arrie,

Suspect that I am writing more letters to you than you appreciate but when I've the time, I am going to write all that I can until you inform me that I must stop.

I would certainly like to be with you this afternoon and talk with you. I look at your picture very often and wonder when I'll be permitted to see you again. I am not going to try to express my feelings to you, in fact, I do not want you to know them but I do want you to know that I am think of you.

I told you that I would not say anything more about love unless you wanted me to, therefore, I must be very careful not to do so. I wish now that I had not said that because it is very hard for me to write you a letter and not express a part of my love to you. I will try to keep my promise, though.

The Companys [sic] of the 18th M.G. Bat. had a contest this forenoon to see which was the most efficient one in the drills, do not know yet which Co. won but I hope that mine did. Landrum is about thirty two miles directly north of Spartanburg.[xvii]

Answer real soon, Yours, Sam Riggins

June 17, 1918
Dear Arrie,

I am going to punish Mr. Smith, this morning by writing another letter to you, it may, also, be a punishment for you, however, I hope not. If I thought that it would be, would not write it but I think that you would inform me, if you wanted me to stop writing so often.

I am on guard today but, am not having a very hard time, therefore, have time to write this letter. I think that, will write a long one.

You said that you very often wondered what I was doing, just imagine that I'm trying to show someone how to use a M.G. [machine gun] effectively and you will have it right, while I'm here. That is, when I am not attending school of some kind. I have been trying to instruct on one of the M.G.'s for the past week and a half. There are thirty of them in one line, you may imagine that they made some noise. I can not hear very well now but as soon as I am away from the guns for awhile, can hear alright.

Sure, I can milk, string beans, mash dishes or do most anything else, there is to do but, do not think that I would like to, am real lazy. I do not like to work, do you? If I have a lot of work to do, I think that, am sick. So, you see, work has an awful effect upon me.

No, I have never said that I hoped Arrie would write a better hand or stop writing either. If I did not want you to write to me I would tell you so, and your hand writing is good. I do not want you to think that I want you to improve your hand writing or stop writing either.

I would certainly enjoy going with you to Sunday School and , am looking forward to the time when I may be permitted to do so. I do not have the opportunity of going to S.S. now but I know that the future will bring different arrangements, and that's about all the consolation that I have. I want you to know that my enjoyment depends upon you. I have nothing else to hope for except you. I am telling you plain facts and you know it as, at least, I think that you do. You are, I might say, everything to me. And I am telling you so, in order that you may not doubt my love for you.

A part of the Sixth Division has gone to France already and we aren't going to have the chance to complete the course, which, we came out here to take, which was a six weeks course.[xviii]

I will stop for fear of waste basket. Yours and yours only, Sam Riggins, Answer soon.

June 23, 1918
Dear Arrie,

Read your letter yesterday and appreciated it very much. I received two from you last week and you know that, was glad to get both of them.

I have just been looking at your picture. I shant send it back to you. Am going to carry it to France with me that's if I go myself. If I thought that, was going I would not be allowed to say anything about it.

My company came second in the contest, which, I told you about.

If I should go to France my address would be Sergeant Sam Riggins, Co. "C" 18th M.G. Bn. A.E.F.

Yours, Sam

Will write every time that I can and, am expecting you to do the same. Sam

P.S. I was not supposed to leave the Co Street but I slipped off to write a line to you.

June 25, 1918
Dear Arrie,

I started a picture of you of the place where I stayed while up at Landrum, hope that you will get it all o.k.

I receive your letter at noon and you know that I was real glad to hear from you. I received the Testament that you sent too. I thank you very much for it.

I do not know what my address is but you may address the next letter to Camp Wadsworth, think that I will get it alright.

Well, I won't ask you to be good until I see you again because I know that you will. I put more confidence in you than you could imagine that I do, otherwise I would not write so much. Just remember that I want you to write real often.

Yours always, Sam

July 5, 1918
Dear Arrie,

Am real well and I hope that you are too. Received your letter, which, was written on the 26th day of June. I was real glad to get it and was also glad to know that you were enjoying yourself.

No, I did not get the letter, you asked me about until on Saturday. I move around so much that, suspect, it is pretty hard for the mail clerks to keep up with me.

I went down to Long Beach yesterday and went in swimming, sure had a first time but got sun burned pretty bad. I wish that you could visit these places up here, think that you would never forget them. The government has been paying our expenses since we arrived here. It did not cost us anything to go to Long Beach yesterday, think that it is trying to make us enjoy ourselves for a few days.

Air planes are plentiful up here, and can see as many as thirty most any time.[xix]

I read a letter from Henry Howard yesterday says that he is having a lot of work to do. I can not sympathize with him but, could if it were drills. I have plenty of drilling to do.

I would have written to you before now but, was not allowed to do so, however, I hope that you will receive this letter. I do not have many privileges when it comes to writing.

Sure I was glad to get back to Wadsworth, even if I did have to hike and sleep in the rain you spoke of but it did not hurt me any. I almost freeze up here, that's the only thing that I dislike about the place. Want to write more but I can't. Yours always, Sam Riggins

Camp Mills, Long Island, N.Y., Answer soon.

July 5, 1918
Dear Arrie,

I have just finished reading your letter, which, was written on July the first, certainly was glad to hear from you. I wrote a letter to you this morning but after receiving yours, am going to write another.

I do not know the Mr. Miller that you spoke of.

You spoke about your letter sounding like nonsense, it sure did not sound that way to me. I try to not be silly but, am afraid that my letters sound that way to you. If you only knew how much I appreciated your letters you would understand me better. I think though, that you understand me pretty well, am glad that you do.

I am on guard now, went on at 11:30 and will be relieved tomorrow at 11:30. I do not care for going on guard, can write to you then.

As I told you before, I am yours and, will remain yours. No matter where I go and what I have to do, I will come back to you. I do not want you to ever think that I am untrue because, can't always write to you when I want to. I am depending upon you and you alone. I will be true to you all of the time.

No, I did not get offended at you for saying what you did about work and laziness. I think that I understand you. You need not be afraid to write anything that you want to. I told you this before.

Yours, Sam

Answer real soon because I never know today where I will be tomorrow and if I did, would want you to write just the same. Sam

P.S. I have had the opportunity of eating home cooking some of the time since arriving here. I like home cooking better than I do army rations.

July 7, 1918
Dear Arrie,

Am writing you to let you know that my address is not what it used to be and, also, to let you know that I'm real well, and I hope that you are too.

You can not imagine how bad I want to see you and talk with you but you know that I am giving America everything that I am but when the war is over, will be just as true to you as I am to America now. I am true to you now but, must stay away from you for awhile.

Awaiting the pleasure of your earliest reply, I am yours, always, Sgt. Sam Riggins, Co. "C" 18th Machine Gun Bn, A.E.F.

August 9, 1918
Dear Arrie,

I hope that this letter won't meet the same fate that all of my previous ones have since I arrived here, they have all been returned to me, for various reasons.

I received your letter last evening, which, you wrote on July 10th and mailed on the 11th, was certainly glad to get it.

I am real well and hope that you are the same. You know that I am always well though. You said that if I were to see you now, I would see a more serious girl than I did when I saw you last. I think that you were serious enough then. You know that I never seem to have a serious thought but really I do have serious thoughts sometimes.

I can't write very much because my letters are censored, yours are not, therefore, will expect you to write long letters.[xx]

Yours always, Sgt. Sam Riggins, Write real soon.

August 18, 1918
Dear Arrie,

The letter that you wrote to me on the 8th of July reached me yesterday and I appreciated it more than you can imagine. I am always glad to hear from you, hope that your will write real often, while I am over here. Will write all that I can to you.

I hope that your eye is all o.k. now, you said that it kept you from attending Church on the 7th of July. I can sympathize with you because I used to keep a stye on one of my eyes pretty near all of the time.

I suspect that Mama thinks that I have forsaken her because every letter that I have written to her in the last month has come back to me. I am going to write her another this afternoon and risk its going to her.

Awaiting the pleasure of your earliest replay, I am still, Yours, Sgt. Sam Riggins

August 22, 1918
Dear Arrie,

Am real well and I hope that you are the same. I want you to write real often, Yours, Sergeant Same Riggins P.S. Please write all letters, that you write to me, with ink.

September 9, 1918
Dear Arrie,

At this time I can hardly write, not that I am sick but , am feeling fine and dandy, hope to tell you the why I cannot write, real soon. I hope that you are real well too. Yours Always, Sgt Sam Riggins, Write real soon

September 11, 1918
Dear Arrie,

Just a line to let you know that, am real well and, hope that you are the same. I have not the time to write but hope to have real soon.

I hope that Mr. Smith will not permit you to jam the red brass, will tell you why sometime. Write real soon, Yours, Sgt. Sam Riggins

September 16, 1918
Dear Arrie,

I received the three letters which you addressed A.E.F. and I sure was delighted to get them, am real well and I hope that you are the same.

No, I have not seen a watermelon in France, or any other eats of that kind. They are not here. I am glad that you have been attending a singing school, want to hear you sing and play when I return.

Yours always, Sergeant Sam Riggins, Write real soon

September 21, 1918
Dear Arrie,

Am now in the front line ditches, writing this letter by a small light, that I burn while in my Dugout. Quite a number of shells and bullets can be heard, whizzing by, therefore, you must not expect a very long letter. I do not want you to keep that idea that you had when you wrote to me last. You said that you were not going to write anymore until you heard from me because it would bother me too much. You may rest assured that every letter that you may write will be appreciated.

Your always, Sgt. Sam Riggins, Please write soon

September 28, 1918
Dear Arrie,

Have just received and read your letter written on the 24th of August, was certainly glad to hear from you. I received the one, which you wrote on August 19th day before yesterday and appreciated it too.

I am real well and, hope that you are the same. I am always real well, you know.

I suspect that you have your watch fixed by this time, hope that you have anyway. I will give you the difference of $2.00 between yours and mine, providing you let your chain stay on the watch you have.

You spoke about attending services. I attended services once while in the front line ditches. So you see that I am not so bad after all of my drills. Probably you think that I am forgetting you, since leaving America. If you do, you are absolutely wrong. Nothing could happen that would cause me to do so, as I told you while there, I never forget a friend of mine.

I have heard no Katydids since I arrived in France, do not think that there's any here.[xxi]

Writing paper sure is hard to get over here, we have to be very conservative with it. Sugar, candy, etc, can hardly be gotten, therefore, we must eat less sweets than we did in America.

Awaiting the pleasure of your earliest reply, I am as ever,

Yours always, Sgt Sam Riggins

September 29, 1918
Dear Arrie,

All of your letters have been received and appreciated very much, am real well and, hope that you are the same.

I am certainly glad that you have attended a Singing School. I am going to ask you to play and sing all the new songs for me, when I return. You know that no one appreciates music more than I.

I am getting plenty to eat over there and am, also, having some fun, you know that I'll have fun if anybody does. But, when I have the chance, you may rest assured that I will return to South Carolina (That's the place for me.) I must stop for now, write real soon and real often. Yours always, Sgt. Sam Riggins

October 1, 1918
Dear Arrie,

The letter, which, you wrote on August the 11th was received last evening and was appreciated too. You hoped that I would get it before Sept 2nd so you see, it was just one month late.

I suppose that your school is progressing nicely by now and, you are fairly well contented, I hope so anyway. I hope that Mr. Smith does permit you to drive that horse that he traded old Bob for because I do not want you to walk to and from school.

You said that you would be my friend as long as I wanted you to be. That being the case, you will always be my friend for I always want you to be.

Arrie, I do not know what to think about my home people, have received only one letter from them since arriving in France. They do not seem to know my address but I have repeatedly sent it to them. The only mail that I get, comes from you sometimes. I wonder if I have no other friend in America. I would like to be a member of your glee club, probably I can jam it when? Yours always, Sgt Sam Riggins, Please write soon

October 19, 1918
Dear Arrie,

Just a line to let you know that I am real well and, hope that you are the same.

I received your letter, written on September 11th and certainly did appreciate it, will answer it as soon as possible. Yours always, Sgt. Sam Riggins, Please write soon

October 20, 1918
Dear Arrie,

I would like to have some papers and magazines to read but I won't ask you to send any. I do not know whether magazines can be delivered or not but I think that they can. No kind of presents can be delivered to me. So, I guess that I will not get any Xmas presents this year.

I do not think that the girls over here are very pretty, although, some of them have blue eyes. I have been to the front and could hear the roar of the cannons, while up there. But, you would naturally know that we would hear the noise of guns while at the front.

Fila Garrison did her fellow in France a favor by marrying, don't you think so to? I would not express my opinion that way to anyone but you, therefore, do not get the idea that I talk about other folks in a disrespectful manner. I am by that like Enos Smith was by the girl that refused his company, no one know it by you, remember?

I hope that Enos will learn to write perfect letters but I doubt if he does, do not think that anyone has ever learned that yet. I am real glad that he is attending school at Six Mile. I think that they have a very good school there.

I have no idea as to when the soldiers over here will arrive back in America. You know more about the war than I do. I hope, however, that it won't be long. With kindest regards, and best wishes, I am, Yours always, Sgt. Sam Riggins, Please write real soon.

October 30, 1918
Dear Arrie,

Have just received you letter written to me on Sept 26 and I was certainly glad to get it. I am real well and, hope that you are the same.

The letter which one of your pupils wrote was fine for such a young boy, hope that you will tell me more about your School next time you write. I am interested in school work.

If you except the invitation to Mr. Gilstrope's wedding, please let me know how well you enjoyed yourself.

I doubt very seriously If I were in S.C. on the night of Sept 23rd, think that I was in a box car riding through France.

Well, I want to tell you that I am still thinking of you and, will continue to do so until I return. I know that you will remember that I am just as true to you as I was while in America. I will give you the three sentences that has been used most by the boys over here. Here they are. I love you, don't marry and pray for me. A Y.M.C.A. Secretary said that the three above sentences had been used more than any other three by the boys over here.

I can not say just how many letters I have received from you but, am pretty sure that I have received all of your letters so far. They are being delivered promptly.

I suspect that mother is better satisfied now. She said that she had go one letter from me since I sailed. I have got one from her. You can't imagine how glad I was to get it.

Please excuse this letter, I mean excuse paper and writing. I have no paper except this and nothing except the ground to write on.

With all of my love and best wishes I am,

Yours always, Sgt. Sam Riggins

Please write real soon and tell me everything that you want me to know, if I have the opportunity, am going to write you a long letter real soon,

Sam R.

November 28, 1918
Dear Arrie,

Am spending a seven day pass at Aix-Les-Raines, one of the finest places that I've seen since I arrived in France. The Hotel in which I'm staying certainly is a beauty. It is known as the Astoria Hotel, wish that you could see it.

I am expecting to sail for America real soon, hope to get there before Xmas but I do not think that will be that lucky. I certain am anxious to see America again but, am more anxious to see you. I certainly would like to talk with you this afternoon. But it is useless for me to tell you that because you know that already. I have just lots to tell you when I see you but, I do not expect to do all the talking, am expecting you to do a great deal of it, think that I had rather hear you talk than to talk myself. With kindest regards and best wishes, I am, Your always, Sgt. Samuel Riggins, Please write soon

November 30, 1918
Dear Arrie,

I wonder what you did for Thanksgiving? I took an hour swim, watched a football game and went to a movie and Vaudeville show.[xxii] I also ate quite a few lunches at the Y.M.C.A. Building. You see, I had a real busy day.

I think that, will take a walk today up to the top of Mount Revard, I will be delighted if you will walk me up there. Its only about twenty one miles, just a short walk, but unfortunately there is snow to be gone through most of the way. The ground has no snow upon it here but this place is enclosed in mountains that are covered with snow. It sure is great to have the opportunity of seeing this one place, hope to tell you about it real soon.

I hope that the influenza has vanished from America by this time.[xxiii] It seems to be worse than the Germans. The cooties are just about as bad, have had plenty of those myself.[xxiv] Ha.Ha. I should not tell you about cooties but everybody over here knows about them, therefore, I guess that its no harm to tell you about them too. I hope not at least. I believe that we Americans call them Lice do we not? With best wishes and kindest regards, I am, Yours always, Sgt. Sam Riggins, Write soon.

December 11, 1918
Dear Arrie,

My pass expires tonight, will start back to my company in about two hours, am anxious to go because I know that will get several letters from you when I get back to it. I have been thinking about you and your letters every day since I came on pass.

The arc which you may see on the opposite side of this sheet and in the left upper corner was built two hundred years before Christ. All the scriptures here are very old. Am sending you a card showing the Hotel in which I have stayed since I arrived here. I must stop and collect my belongings, Yours always, Sgt. Sam Riggins, Write real soon.

December 12, 1918
Dear Arrie,

I received three letters from you on last Friday when I returned back from Aix-Les-Bains, was certainly glad to get all of them.

You made mention of the fact that I have not been answering all of your questions but I have answered all that I could, will try to do better now. I have more time you see. I received the letter that you spoke of that contained the questions. I answered all of them that I could, all that the Censor would let me answer. Evidently, you have not received the answers.

Sure, I always like Dexter Jones, think that he's a fine guy. I am real glad that he is in the Training Camp.

I was real sorry to hear that Mr. Clark was dead, am not much of a fellow to express my opinion of people whom I know very little about but I judged him to be one of the finest men that I ever met, am not saying this just because he's dead but that's the opinion that I formed of him.

I must stop for now. Yours always, Sgt. Sam Riggins, Please write soon.

P.S. I wrote several letters to you not long ago and all of them returned to me, you may imagine that I am not pleased about it very much.

December 13, 1918
Dear Arrie,

Would like very much to be back in S. C. now but doubtless you know that already. Nothing would please me more right now that to have the opportunity of being with you, but as can not will take the pleasure of writing a letter to you.

Did Mr. Smith trade that Halter of when he traded old Bob?[xxv] I hope that he did. It certainly was a puzzle for me and, is yet. I never did learn how to operate it.

I received three letters from home the other day. You know that I appreciated them, have received very few letters from home since I arrived in France. Most all of my letters have been from you.

I am sorry that you could not pick as much cotton as some of your brothers and sisters could, not that I cared whether you were a fast cotton picker or not but you said that it worried you because you could not. I do not like for you to be worried.[xxvi]

Yours always, Sgt. Sam Riggins, Write real quickly.

December 15, 1918
Dear Arrie,

Just a line to let you know that I am real well and, hope that you are the same.

I suppose that the weather is real cold in S.C. now. No ice is to be found at any where now. On the 12th of October I was in a different part of France and it was snowing there at that time, will tell you the part that I was in when I see you. One thing that I dislike very much and that is the fact that it's very seldom clear here. Most of the time it is damp and foggy. With kindest regards and best wishes, am still yours,

Sgt. Sam Riggins, Answer quickly please.

December 16, 1918
Dear Arrie,

I may be writing more letters to you than you appreciate, however, I hope not. I told you when I saw you last that I was going to write real often, when it was possible, am fulfilling my promise or rather doing what I said that I would.

I noticed this forenoon that Mr. Wilson was in Paris now, would like to see him myself while he's over here but do not think that I'll have the opportunity of doing so.[xxvii]

I have received no mail from you in about a week. Am expecting a letter real soon from you, hope to get it tomorrow.

I know that all of your people over there are planning for a fine Xmas. I sure would like to be there with you. I would show you how your red headed soldier could enjoy himself. But, the wine will soon come when you and I will have the chance of hearing each other talk, you can't imagine how I am longing for that time to come.

I will stop before I express my feelings to much. If I was with you, would not mind telling you about my feelings but if I write them you will think that I am silly. As ever, Yours, Sgt. Sam Riggins, Please write soon.

February 11, 1919
Dear Arrie,

I have been away from my company for the last month and a half, attending a M. G. School. Consequently I had no one to censor my letters. Therefore, do not think that it was my fault because you have received no mail from me. I was delighted to get several of your letters yesterday when I arrived back to my company. I am real sorry though that you have been sick, hope that you are feeling fine again.

I am sick and have been for several days, have not been to the hospital but the doctor said that I ought to go. I do not know that this letter will be sensible or readable but am doing the best that I can.

Yes, I heard that Mr. Grave was dead, also, heard that several others were dead, think that I won't find all of my friends when I return to S. C. but, then I should not worry so much as I do. I think that I worry too much about friends some times but one cannot always help it.

I do not understand why you said that you were willing to stop writing when I was but, will not ask you to tell me until I see you. I hope that it is nothing that I've said or done. If so, would like to know when I see you. I am just like this about it, am yours, always just like I told you before and I want you to be mine, however, that is all up to you. Will write to you again tomorrow, can not write any more just now.

Yours always, Sgt. Samuel L. Riggins, Please write soon.

February 12, 1919
My dear Arrie,

Am feeling quite a bit better today but I am not feeling well yet. I hope that this will find you in the very best of health and having all the fun that you wish to have.

I am sorry that I cannot tell you why the letters U.S.A. appears in the upper left hand corner of all envelopes addressed to you from overseas. I did not know that those letters were supposed to be there.

I am sending a little souvenir to you, would send you a nice Birthday present but I am in a small isolated place where nothing can be bought that is worth sending to you. I am going to try to find a real nice present for you before I return. ~~To you~~.

Well, we soldiers over here are having some real cold weather now, snow has been on the ground for about two weeks ~~now~~. But, the sun is shining this morning and it is not so unpleasant as it has been. I suppose that you are having some cold weather in S.C. now but I hope that you do not have to stay out in it as much as I do.

I would like to present to you a real picture of France. No doubt you would change your mind about it. I think that most folks over there thinks that we have a wonderful place to stay while over here, they have it right to believe me. Everything over here is all the way behind things in America. The people are dirty, I don't think some of them ever washed their faces. I can't tell you about the [reason] now [why] my letter would not pass the Censor but, will tell you when I see you.

With kindest regards and best wishes, I am Yours always, Sgt Sam Riggins, Write real soon please.

February 13, 1919
My dear Arrie,

I wrote a letter to you on the 11th but I notice that it is still here in the orderly room. I also, wrote one yesterday that has already started on its way to you. I hope that you will soon receive both of them and this one too. I am feeling lots better today almost fell strong again, hope that you are real well.

No, I was not among the boys that paraded before Mr. Wilson, think that they were all Engineers from the 318th.[xxviii] I mean the ones from my division. You asked me if I would teach French to you when I returned. If you knew just how much I have learned you would be surprised. I possibly have learned a dozen words. I do not want to learn it, these French people make me sick muttering away all the time. Nothing is more provoking than to go up to one of these French ladies and ask for something to eat and then have to listen to her long tongue, wish that you could hear them once.

I will be delighted to visit your school when I get back but do not think that, can tell any experiences that will interest you or your pupils, neither can I teach. Ha.Ha. I suspect that you are deciding that I can't do anything but you know I must always try, that's all anyone can do.

I doubt, if the George Washington brought you a letter from me, because I was away to school. I told you about it in my letter dated the 11th of February. Sure, I will try to sing for you the songs, which you asked me to sing for you, sometime this Spring, I hope. I will have to ask you to play them though. My voice is almost gone just now but, hope that it will be strong by that time. I am going to ask you to sing for me all the new songs that you have, think that we will be even then. I am not going to forget the talk either. Am just crazy to hear you talk. I know that you have just lots to tell me. I will promise to tell you all that I can about France, etc.

I hope to arrive there just about the time that Strawberries get ripe, do not think that I will ever forget last year when the Strawberries were ripe, do you? I only hope that you enjoyed yourself as much as I did. Do not forget that I am just as true to you now as was when I left.

Yours still and always, Sgt. Sam Riggins, Answer real soon please.

February 17, 1919
My dear Arrie,

Just a few lines to let you know that I am all O.K. and hoping that you are too.

I am in luck this week. My company has gone out to maneuvers for the entire week and I am left behind in charge of The Bath House, pretty easy for me is not it? But, then, the weather isn't very cold just now, it would not be so bad you know. I do not mind the drills if the weather is favorable but, sure do not like the idea of drilling in the rain and snow.

I wonder just what you did yesterday, suspect though that you attended Church at Gloucester, sure wish that I could have gone with you.[xxix] But, probably you enjoyed yourself better than you would if I had been with you, however, I hope that you will enjoy my company when I arrive there, know that I will enjoy yours, if you will permit me to do so.

I am expecting that letter telling me all about the Columbian Community. You said that you would write and tell me all the news that Ethel Smith brought to you if it was interesting, you need not worry but what I'll be interested in anything that you may wish to write to me.

Suspect, that I had better stop, if I want this to pass the Censor and I certainly do, because it is quite a job to get mail censored just now.

With best wishes and kindest regards, I beg to remain your Sam Riggins, Write soon please.

February 28, 1919
Dear Arrie,

Am sending you three post cards, which were taken near where I am now located, will send more later, do not think that I can send very many in one letter.

I have just read a list of the Divisions, that are to sail for America before the 1st of July, am real sorry to say that the 6th was not included. Suppose that I will be over here for some time yet.

Well, it will soon be time for me to take another pass, and believe me I am going to take it, if nothing prevents, think that I will go to Scotland, come over and go with me. I think that you would enjoy seeing some of the old countries, would not you?

I will make this letter short because we have no officers to censor mail except one from another company. Ours have gone to school.

Yours always, Sgt. Sam Riggins, Please write quickly.

March 3, 1919
Dear Arrie,

With great pleasure, I received and read your letter dated February 10th and am answering it at the first possible moment. One of your letters dated January 31st reached me three weeks after you wrote it. I hope that this one will reach you that quick but, doubt if it does.

No, nothing dreadful has happened to me, although, I have not felt well since the first of January but, think that I will if the sun ever shines any and it stops raining a few days. You may expect rain ever six hours over here, however, I hope that these conditions will improve with the coming Spring.

I received the letter with the chewing gum in it and I want you to know that, was delighted to get it, also, that which came in todays letter. I will always be glad to get anything that you may wish to send to me. Especially, a letter.

You spoke of going to Winthrop this summer, hope that you do because it will give you a rest and then one never regrets the time, which, they spend in school. I would like to attend school myself but the Army will keep me I suppose until my hair is gray, it looks that way now at least. I would give anything that I have to be out of the Army just at this time.

You said that I might not be interested in farm work. You can bet your life that I am. I have been under bosses until I'm tired of it. I want to be free all the time after I get out from under my present bosses. I think that the farm is the only place to be free, do not you?

Well, I do not know anything of interest to write, therefore, will stop for now.

Yours always, Sgt. Sam Riggins

P.S. I suppose that, will have to write the same thing in my next letter to you, wish that you knew just how scarce news is over here. I could write lots but you would wonder why I wrote it because it is all same thing that would not interest you or at least I do not believe that it would. I have a hard time trying to think of something to write Mother that she really is glad to know. I am afraid to write for fear you will get tired reading the same thing over and over again. If I knew that you would be half as glad to know the happenings over here as I am to know them over there, would write you a letter every day.

S.R., Please write real quick.

March 4, 1919
My dear Arrie,

Am taking the pleasure of writing you another letter, which, I hope that you will soon get. I am not hardly so homesick today as usual, but still have a bad case. Did you ever get homesick when you were at college? I hope that you will not get that way this summer, if you decide to go back to Winthrop.

Arrie, when you see anything interesting in the papers over there, please, cut it out and send it to me, will send you same clippings from the papers over here if I can find any that I think will interest you.

Say, I still have the picture which you sent to me while I was at Wadsworth and believe me, am going to keep it. I carried it through the front line trenches and all through the Argonne Forest, but it still resembles you very much. I also, have one of my sister, Mary, which, I expect to keep.

I received a letter from Matt Davis last week saying that a number of soldiers had already gotten home from France and had been discharged. They sure are lucky, I think. But, then, it is pretty hard to cross the

Atlantic when it is cold. You see I do not like cold weather very much. I must stop and go to non com's school.[xxx]

Write real quickly, Yours still and always, Sgt. Sam Riggins

March 24, 1919
Dear Arrie,

Am in the hospital and I have been for two weeks. Would have written you sooner but I did not want you to know that I am sick. I hope that this will find you in the best of health and enjoying life in every way possible.

I am expecting to attend the Beaune University If I can ever get able but I never will so long as it rains and stays cloudy.[xxxi] I am positive that nothing else is the matter with me. We do not have weather here like you people have over there. I believe that I gave you an idea of the weather here in one of my previous letters, did I not?

Will send to you a couple of clippings from the Stars and Stripes, which I intended to have sent earlier but, have not written any letters lately. I hope that you can read them even if they are wrinkled from being carried in my pocket. With kindest regards and best wishes, I am as ever,

Yours always, Sgt. Sam Riggins, Please write quickly.

March 30, 1919
Dear Arrie,

I am feeling much better than, was when I wrote you last. I hope that this will find you real well and having all the pleasure that anyone can possible have. I did not tell you in my last letter what my trouble was. I have not trouble except for breathing, once quite a bit of trouble breathing this damp air at times, while at other times I can breathe fine, comparatively speaking. I do not know what the Doctors are going to do with me. I hope, however, that they will send me some place where the climate suits me better.

I suppose that you have decided by this time what you are going to do after the preparation of your school, hope that you have decided to attend Winthrop because you may get a rest in that way, that is if you do not study too much. Am sure that I would not if I were going.

Do you know anything about Henry Howard? I have not heard from him in sometime. You know Henry is a special friend of mine and, would like to get in touch with him again.

Hoping to get an early reply, I am yours always, Sgt. Sam Riggins

April 13, 1919
Dear Arrie,

Am at [Brest, France], think that, will be at same before very long. Am on my way now.

As ever, Sam Riggins

April 17, 1919

Dear Arrie,

I am now at hospital 120 but, do not think that I will be here very much longer. Possibly, I will sail for America toot sweet.[xxxii]

As ever, Sgt. Sam Riggins

May 22, 1919
Dear Arrie,

The headlines on paper will show to you where I am now at, do not know just how long that I will be here but have an idea that it won't be very long.

I am real nervous as you can see by my marking, therefore, will give you my address and stop for now.

Yours always, Sgt. Sam Riggins

May 29, 1919

My dear Arrie,

Had just finished writing a letter to you when yours came, in fact I had not sealed the envelope, therefore, I will just tear the old letter up and write ~~a new one~~ another. I was so glad to hear from you, I just can't tell you how I feel just now but I do not feel sick in the least, neither do I feel blue, was feeling just a letter blue until your letter came. I had received no mail from you since March the 1st. You may imagine how anxious I was to hear from you.

I will now tell you my trouble or the reason that I am here. I had a nervous breakdown or that is what the Doctors have on my clinical record, caused from over work they say. I do not know what caused it but I know that was awfully nervous you know. I was always a little nervous, am getting alright now think that I am so more nervous now than before I went to the army, do not know how I will be after I start to work again. Have done nothing since March the 13th that day that I went to the Hospital. I do not think that work had very much to do with my getting nervous anyway. Think that it was caused mostly by my not being able to hear from you and have very often have not heard from home now since long before I heard from you last. Don't know whether papa and mama have moved to Greenville or not. I know that they have been writing to me but my being away from any Co most of all the time prevented my getting it. At any rate I know that I felt fine when the war was over.

No, I have heard nothing from Henry Howard since I left for France. Do not know where he is, would certainly like to hear from him, probably. I will be able to get in touch with him now.

I am glad that your school is out because I know that you need a rest. Hope too that you will take me. I do not want you to meet with the same fate that I have. I know that you have worked just as hard during the war as I have and that is why I want you to rest all summer. I would have been ever so glad to have seen you teach some before your school closed but I just could not get there in time.

From here I will go to Camp Jackson and then home, think that I will be there in about two weeks.[xxxiii] Say, Arrie, I have just been wondering if the Strawberries were ripe. You remember they were when you and I were together last. Believe me, I have not forgotten that time. I do not know why but life does not seem real to me when I can't see or hear from you. All of my pleasures are gone when I am away from you. I am certainly glad that I am soon to see and hear you talk again. You bet, it is fine to be back in America again where I can hear from you real often.

Well, I must stop writing and reread your letter. Am afraid that I was all excited when I got it and did not understand all of it. I just hurried to finish reading it so that I could get an answer made and started on it way to you. You see, I am real [anxious] to hear from you again and the sooner you hear from me the sooner you can answer.

As ever, yours, Sgt. Samuel Riggins

P.S. I am going to mail this right now and am going to ask you to answer it just as soon as you receive it.

June 1, 1919
My dear Arrie,

Received your letter written on May the 27th and 28th. I was certainly glad to get it but, was sorry that your mouth was sore, hope that it has gotten alright by now. I do not know of a thing that is good for a sore mouth but, hope that you found something that cured it.

I do not know what to say about the League of Nations but, I think that the whole world would be much better off if it could take the League out in some quiet spot and bury it.[xxxiv] I won't try to tell you why I think so until I see you. Please give me your opinion in your next letter. I do not know whether or not Germany will sign the Peace Terms but think that it makes very little difference because Germany is absolutely helpless.

I got a pass and went to Norfolk day before yesterday and yesterday attended a Field Meet so you see that I do not have to be in bed.

I received a letter from Papa stating that he had moved to Greenville and was getting along fine, was glad to hear from him, you know, and to know that my people were all well.

I want to get this off on the morning's mail so will stop by asking you to send and early reply to your, Sam Riggins

June 5, 1919
My dear Arrie,

Am all disgusted, was expecting to get home real soon but now I do not know when will get there. Am under quarantine on account of Diphtheria.[xxxv] I hope that no one else takes it.

Received your 3rd letter, written to me since I arrived back in America. Was certainly glad to get it. I want to thank you for the cake, it sure was fine. You can hardly imagine how much I enjoyed eating it.

Arrie when I get home I am not going to wait for your permission to call and see you. Am to anxious to see you for that. Possibly, I had better ask you in this letter whether I may come right on over and see you or not? Please tell me in your reply to this letter.

I will have to stop for now because a show is almost ready to start in the Red Cross Hut.[xxxvi] Will write you again tomorrow.

Ever Yours, Sgt. Samuel Riggins

June 6, 1919
My dearest Arrie,

How are you feeling today? I am real well but, am not enjoying myself one bit, hope that you are well and having all the pleasure that it is possible for anyone to have.

If no more patients takes Diphtheria I will go to Camp Jackson Monday next but if they do I do not know when will go.

You said that the letters which you received from me while I was in France did not seem like my letters. I do not suppose that they did, have not been myself since I left you one year ago. You mean more to me than anything that the world contains just can not live without you. Have tried awfully hard to be contented away from you but it is impossible. Without you I have no desire to live. You may say that I am weak minded else would not be that way. Well I maybe, have no control of myself in that respect. Whatever, have tried to put my mind on something else but can't do it. I can think of other things but still, am thinking of you at the same time, have no doubt but what that is one of the curses of my nervousness. While in France I saw the condition that was getting in and tried every way that I knew to keep from getting in the condition that am now in but failed. I will now tell you why you did not receive letters from me at times when you that that I should write. I thought that if I did not write to you that possible could keep from thinking of you all the time but instead I go all the worse that is I thought of you night and day, could not sleep nor eat very much. I just cannot write all that, want to, will try to explain myself to you when I arrive there if you'll listen to me.

Yours always, Sgt Sam Riggins, Answer soon.

June 7, 1919
My dear Arrie,

Am now at New-Port-News on pass and I am feeling fine. Hope that you are feeling the same. I was real glad when the Surgeon told me that the quarantine was off until someone else took some contagious disease.

I expected a letter from you today but was disappointed, it never came, hope that one comes tomorrow for I am real anxious to hear from you again I have received only four letters since I arrived from overseas. One from papa and three from you.

I had charge of a detail today that did just a little bit of work, the first duty that we done for the last three months, think that I am going to be real strong now, I weigh 155 lbs and feel strong. I must stop and go back to camp. My pass is almost up.

Yours, Sam Riggins, Please write soon

June 11, 1919

My dear Arrie,

Just when I will get away from this place I do not know, am still under quarantine and it looks now like that I will be for some time. Some one always has to get sick or do something else to spoil ones pleasure while he's in the army.

I would enjoy writing if could write a good hand but you know that I can't and never could write a good one. I will have to get you to teach me how to write and also how to speak English. If I ever know anything about books, have forgotten all of it. But, am willing to learn.

I do not know just how you expect me to write a long letter when I know nothing to write that would interest you. I know that you are not anxious to know how hot the weather is up here and what I am doing because you know already what one has to do while under quarantine. I know again that you do not care to know that about 2000 patients are at this place. So, you see I know of nothing at all to write that is interesting. I would have enjoyed going to the S.S. (Sunday School) with you ever so much. Are you going to let me go, after I arrive home, I mean to go with you? Possibly I can soon learn how to conduct myself at S.S. (Sunday School) and Church. Those are the two places that I am anxious to learn about.

I will try to write to you real often but do not think that can think of very much to write at any one time.

Ever yours, Sgt. Samuel Riggins, Please answer quickly

June 12, 1919
My dear Arrie,

Won't you talk to me just a little this afternoon? I would be ever so glad if you would, am certainly lonesome and blue, just don't know what to do. Were you ever lonesome and blue? I hope that because one had better be sick don't you think? Waiting is going to make me feel good until I see you and then I think that my enjoyment will be complete. You may expect me to call at your home at any time after I leave here, am going to visit you the first possible moment.

I have no photo of any French girls you know it. The only photos that I have is one of yours and one of my sisters. I will not and have not loved any girl except you, am just as true to you as I was before I left America. Of course, you know it else you would not write to me. I would not want you to write to me if you thought that I loved some other girl. I do not want you to ever let me come into your presence unless you think that I am perfectly clean. I will never put myself where you will have to speak to me if you do not think so. I love you much, better than anything that I know of but I do not ask you to even associate with me unless you are willing to trust me at all times. If I thought that you loved some other boy better than me and trusted him more than you do me, would let you go with that boy and would not trouble you in the least. I write to you because I love and trust you, if I were not willing to trust you and did not love you, am sure that you would never get another letter from me. Please write real soon to your, Sgt. Sam Riggins

P.S. Will try to let you know when I am going to visit you.

June 17, 1919
My dear Arrie,

Have just received your letter written to me yesterday and, I am answering it at the first possible moment. I hope that this will find you enjoying the very best of health, am feeling fine myself but, am far from being happy. I used to think that I would never worry but, have reached the conclusion now that here is not a person living that worries more than I. Anyone knows that he should not worry but still he will very often do it.

I have no idea just how long that it will take me to learn how to conduct myself properly at S.S. (Sunday School) and Church but hope that it will not take very long. If I can just get the army and army affairs off of my mind, will have no trouble whatever.

Say, I was looking at your photo when your letter arrived today, even tho it is worn and scratched, I am going to keep it always if possible. Am sorry that I have not been able to take better care of it but you know that it has been hard for me to keep anything in good condition.

No, I will not leave the hospital now until I get permission to do so, have nothing against me so far and am going out of the army with a clean record if some officer does not say something that I dislike. The quarantine has been lifted and I am now on a list that should have gone to Atlanta to-day but the shortage of transportation prevented me going, they say that is the reason that we did not go. I do not think that they are trying very hard to get us any place. If they were I do not think that they would be constantly changing the passenger lists do you? I have not the least idea how long I will have to stay in Ft. McPherson, in fact, am so disgusted that I do not try to find out anything.[xxxvii]

If this letter does not reach you "toot sweet" you need not answer it until you hear from me again. Will let you know all that I can about myself until I see you.

As ever, yours, Sgt. Sam Riggins

June 20, 1919
Dear Arrie,

Am riding at a fine speed on my way to McPherson. I will arrive there tomorrow at 6 o'clock. Ah! But it is nice to ride on an American train especially in America, will write to you immediately after I get off the train.

As ever, Sam R.

June 22, 1919

Dear Arrie. Am now in Atlanta but I am not discharged. Will have to report to McPherson this evening, do not know when I will be discharged, am marked duty and have an idea this it won't be long.

Sam R.

June 24, 1919
My dear Arrie,

Am real well and I hope that you are the same, have just completed my days work of about fifteen minutes exercise, think that I will go to Atlanta this afternoon and break the monotony of hospital life. Was up there last evening but on account of rain I stirred around very little. All of we invalid soldiers get free tickets to the Rialto and Forsyth Theatres and naturally one would pretty near always find us at one of the two places when we are in Atlanta.

The doctors wanted to send me from here to Jackson for demobilization but I kept insisting that I be demobilized at Yarden until finally they agreed to send me but to Yarden. Am so anxious to get out that I do not want to be shipped around any more than is absolutely necessary. It does seem to me that I'm having one hard time getting out of the army. Do not think that I'll ever have anything to do with another one if I'm ever discharged out of this one. I'll write you again real soon. As ever,

Yours, Sgt Sam Riggins, General Hospital #6, Ft. McPherson, Ga.

June 25, 1919
My dear Arrie,

I started a couple of souvenirs on their way to you this forenoon, hope that you will get them all O.K. They are not what I wanted to send you but I had no chance to buy anything after I go into hospital. Am real well and I hope that you are the same.

I went to Atlanta yesterday and had a very nice time but nothing to compare with the time that I expect to have with you within the very near future. Am going to listen to you talk just as long as you will talk to me.

I very often wonder if you really know just how much love that I have for you and just what you mean to me sometimes. I think that you do. During my stay away from you, have thought of you and loved you constantly. Really I just cannot express my love to you but through all the reminder of my life will argue to you that nothing in this world is so dear to me as you.

As ever, yours, Sgt. Sam Riggins

P.S. No, I did not think that you [thought] that I ~~was~~ had any French girls' picture. I have an idea that you know me better than that.

June 28, 1919
My dear Arrie,

If nothing breaks bigger than a shoe string I will be able to see you on Wednesday next. I signed my discharge just a few moments ago but, cannot get it until Monday evening but am going to try to get home Tuesday. You bet that I feel fine now. I hope that you feel the same way.

Hoping to see you Wednesday, I remain, As ever, Sam

July 6, 1919
My dearest Arrie,

Just a few lines to let you know my address and also let you know that I am real well after my first days work. I hope that this will find you real well and happy too. I believe that you said that you were going to be happy, did you not?

I told you that I was coming to Conestee on next Sunday morning but you know that is an awful long time from now, and I would be ever so glad if you had some teeth, which were not decayed, but had to be fixed on Saturday afternoon.[xxxviii] I am not going to work any after noon time on Saturday unless I loose sometime between now and then and naturally I will go to the Main city as quickly after dinner as can of course, you know that I'll have to get my best clothing on before I can go but think that I could make excellent time if, knew that you would be at the Greenville at that time. Please, let me know if you think that you will come to Greenville Saturday afternoon and, am sure that I'll be there if you are. In case you see me in Greenville or any other place ~~you~~ where I do not see you, please [holler] or do something so that I may see you. I will be delighted I you will.

I hope that you can read this scratching. I do not think that I could but you know that I can't write, therefore, I will expect you not to think of poor writing very much. I know that you have never let me know that you cared whether I could write or not. Please answer soon,

Your, Sam R.

July 15, 1919
My dearest,

I have just been wondering whether or not your school started today and really, I hope not because it has been to hot for you to teach. I understood that you were going to try to be lazy all this summer and I was in hopes that you would take a rest whether you succeeded in being lazy or not.

I have just received a picture that one of my friends sent to me. I believe that I'll mail it to you. He took it just before I left Newport News. You have several photos of myself but then if you get over stocked ~~they~~ it will not be hard for you to destroy part of them.

Arrie, I am in just a little hurry this evening and if you'll promise to excuse me I'll go play under the shower before the water is turned off. I will [write] more next time. Yours, Sam

July 23, 1919
Thursday 8 PM

My dearest,

Have just finished reading your letter and I was certainly glad to receive it. Am real well and hope that you are the same.

I would like very much to help you eat cantaloupes and grapes, sure enjoyed eating those last Sunday. But is all depends upon the person that I am with whether I enjoy eating so well or not. Several times in my life I have had the very best eats that one could possibly have, set before me but I could not enjoy eating one bit, so you see it is not eating that brings the most enjoyment to some folks, especially myself. I do enjoy eating very much though but enjoy myself better when eating with you than anyone else.

I do not care whether you ever get interested in your teaching or not, in fact, I hope that you won't because I know that you will work hard enough at it without being interested. There is no person that likes working people better than I but you see I have a reason for not wanting you to work so hard teaching. You know what my reason is, am sure.

I hope that you'll be able to read these hurriedly written lines.

Yours, Sam

[P.S.] I wrote to Henry and invited him to the Singing Sunday but doubt very seriously whether he comes or not. He is liable to come too because he thinks, and so does his wife, that you and I are going to get married real soon, and he may think that it will be Sunday if he does am sure that he will be present otherwise, do not think that he will. I'll tell you everything that I know if you wish. Henry's wife gave me a special invitation to bring you up their home after next June. She thinks that there's no girl like yourself. So do I.

July 30, 1919
Wed. 9 PM

My dearest,

Have just returned from Henry's and not very much to my surprise had three letters awaiting me, written by you on March 11, 12, 17th. I was real glad to get them even I they had been to France and back. Am real well and I hope that you are too.

Arrie, if you were not teaching these hot days I would be much better satisfied, do not know how you keep from getting sick. I do not think that, could stand it at all.

It seems to me that ~~it~~ over a week has passed since I saw you last and here it is only Wednesday. Am real anxious for the time to come when I can see you every day. I wonder if you're as anxious to see me right at this time as I am to see you? I realized sometime ago that, could not get along without you. I realize it more and more everyday.

I am certainly trying to write this letter rapidly, not that I want to get thru with it so quickly but the lights will be turned out right way.

Yours always, Sam

P.S. Will see you Sunday afternoon if, not at Sunday School Sunday morning.

August 3, 1919

My dearest,

Have just arrived in Greensville and I am feeling fine hope that you are too.

If you wish I will only be to glad to call at your home on next Sunday PM. I am awfully sorry that you think that I was not at myself this afternoon but, will ask you to just remember that I'll always be yours, no matter how I may act at times. I was real sorry too that you asked me to do something I could not do just before we reached your home but will promise to please you near as possible at all times. I am writing this in the hopes that you'll get it tomorrow.

Yours always, Sam

P.S. I knew that some mistakes will be found on the opposite side of sheet but you know I am doing this hurriedly.

Yours, S.R.

August 5, 1919
Tuesday 8 PM

My dearest,

Have just received and read your letter written yesterday, was real glad to get it and I enjoyed reading it immensely. Am find and dandy. I hope that you are enjoying the very best of health too.

I wrote a letter to you Sun. night after I arrived in Greenville. Suspect that you received it today, hope tho that it reached you yesterday. I told you that I would be only to glad to visit you on next Sunday afternoon, would like very much to attend preaching this week at Conestee but you know that I can't. I started or rather made some effort to come last evening but found that, was going to be later than I thought and did not get there.

Arrie, this is all the paper that I have but you told me sometime ago to make not apologies for paper or bad writing, therefore, will say no more about either at present.

Arrie, will you or can you with me to Liberty on Saturday before the 3rd Sunday and attend the Liberty Township Singing Convention on the 3rd Sunday and know, I will not be offended in the least if you fail to go but, am asking you in time for you to write and get a reply from anyone that you may wish to spend the night with. Then, if you go we will have the entire Sunday to talk. I know that girls cannot do like boys and if your father has any objections whatever, I won't ask you to go.

It is dark and the lights are out, I must stop. Yours, Sam

P.S. I received five letters from you yesterday that had been to France and back. They contained some paper clippings. Sam R.

August 12, 1919
Tuesday PM

My dearest,

I hope that you're feeling as well as I am just at this time and enjoying life just as much. I do think that life was never any more appreciated by anyone than by myself since you have promised to be mine always. My one ambition now is to make you happy and enjoy every moment of your life. I never made any promises before asking you to be mine but I'll promise now that I'll always strive to make you enjoy yourself in every way possible. Am sure that it will always be a pleasure for me to do so.

I have just been eating a part of a watermelon, won't you have some with me? What you and I are going to do when watermelons and grapes are gone, I do not know. But, then the weather will be cold pretty soon and we could not get them in case they were not all gone. Say, you must please let me know when you are going to get your little vacation. Possibly I can ~~get~~ have the opportunity of being with you a start of it. Hoping to get an early reply, I am as ever,

Yours always, Sam

P.S. Are you coming to town on next Saturday? Excuse me for being inquisitive but I want to see you in case you come.

S.R.

August 14, 1919
Thursday 8 PM

My dearest,

Have just received and read your letter. I was delighted to get it, am real well and I hope that you are too.

If it suits you just as well for me to attend the Convention on next Sunday. I will attend. Will write later and let you know when I'll call at your home or rather ask for your permission to call and see you.

As ever, yours, Sam Riggins

August 18, 1919

My dearest,

Never in my life did I enjoy myself better than while was with you yesterday. If I only knew that you enjoyed yourself as well as I, but then you told me that your happiness was almost complete so why should I worry? After you told me that you were happy tho you accused me of being piggish and was afraid that someone would get sick. Maybe I thought that, was not pleasing you all the while and decided to give you a Sunday's rest or as many as you want.

You told me to wait patiently until next June. You know that, can't be patient tho. I have to wait. But I'll promise to do the very best that I can. Will write you again next week.

As ever, yours always, Sam, Please write soon.

August 25, 1919
Monday 11:30 AM

My dearest,

Have just arrived back from Liberty, Jim's watch was slow yesterday and caused me to miss the train, enjoyed myself fine while there wish that you could have been with me. Went to church three times and naturally you know that I'm feeling dine this forenoon.

Next Friday is papa's Birthday and I understand that all of his boys and girls are going to be here. I also understand that Prof. Balding, Mr. Davis and family, Mr. Nathan Smith, and I no. of others are going to be here. Oh! My! How I wish that you could come too. If your school would just close one day sooner, maybe you would. Suspect that we'll spend most of the day in singing, talking and eating.

Arrie there's going to be an unveiling of some kind at Reunion on next Sunday, I promised to be there. If I knew that my asking would not be in vain, would ask you to go with me or rather go and let me go with you.

I must stop and go to work. Yours always, Sam

Answer soon

September 1, 1919
Monday 9:00 pm

My dearest,

I got up this morning feeling fine and dandy and have felt that way since. I hope that you are feeling fine too. I have no reason to feel bad when I have a girl like you. Ah! How I would like to see you right now.

Am sorry that I'm not going to have the opportunity of being with you any this week but just can't help it.

I wrote a letter to the Ruebush Kieffer Co. just a few minutes ago and think that I'll get a replay this week. If I do, will let you know Sunday whether I will go to school or not.[xxxix]

Arrie, I would like to tell you in this letter just how much I love you ~~but,~~ I feel like talking you see, but time and space prevents. I am longing for the time to come when I can sit and tell you in part of my love for you. I am glad that I really love you and don't have to tell stories about it. I love to tell you about my thoughts now since you have promised to let me be yours all the time. And always too. Wishing you the sweetest dreams and the best of sleep tonight.

I am your Sam, Answer soon please

September 9, 1919
Monday 7:00 PM

My dearest,

Have just received and read an answer from the letter which I wrote to Mr. J. H. Ruebush but I got not information of any kind. Will be glad to tell you about it on next Sunday afternoon while I am with you.

How did you enjoy your school work today? I know though that you enjoyed fine because you have already told me that you had rather teach than to do anything that you know of but you know I am not contented unless I ask a lot of questions.

Arrie, I do not understand what you meant when you asked me to help you wait until next June. Tell me in what way that I may help you. I will be only to glad to do it. Have an idea that I know but, am afraid that I do not, therefore, will ask you to explain thoroughly, please.

I don't know exactly why but I thought Sunday night that you had something that you wanted to say to me but for some reason did not. Tell me was I right or wrong? Yours always, Sam Riggins

September 15, 1919
Monday 7:15 PM

My dearest,

With great pleasure I am starting to write a letter to you and inform you that, I am fine and dandy, hope that you are the same. I also hope that your father said nothing to you about my staying there so late last night. Personally, I do not care if I did stay until it was late because I love you and like to be with you, have never regretted any time that I've spent with you, last night included. But, impersonally, I may regret that I stayed so late because I might have made you feel unpleasant today. However, I hope not.

Arrie, I suppose that I've at last become satisfied, in a way for you to track your school until it closes. I suspect or rather know that I'm silly else I would not want you to quit after promising to teach. I can be good alright especially when I have you to make me be that way. I really want to be but last night I felt different. I wonder if you blamed me for it? Anyway, you must make me be good while I'm with you. I don't mean by that that you must take all of, as you say, my privileges away from me. Yours always, Sam Riggins

September 22, 1919
Monday 7:00 PM

My dearest,

I hope that you are well and are having all the pleasures that life can afford anyone. I am feeling exceedingly well and, am enjoying myself in most every way that I know of.

I looked for you Saturday evening until I learned that you had gone from town, do not know why I could not see you anywhere possibly, I will learn sometime.

Mary and Mama are asking an awful lot of questions, am liable to get some of the answers in this letter. If I do you need not be surprised.

Please answer soon to, to your Sam Riggins

October 1, 1919
Wednesday 7:00 AM

My dearest,

Just a few lines, am real well and I hope that you are the same.

Arrie, if you have nothing else to do Saturday evening I will be ever so glad if you will stay in town until about three o'clock, am real anxious to see you again. If you can't please write and tell me whether or not you will be at the Convention Sunday. If you are not going to be there I will be glad to call at your home and see you and if you are, will just as glad to see you at the Convention.

The car is coming therefore I must stop. Yours, Sam

October 27, 1919

Dearest,

Having no paper but his I'm forced to use it. I know that you'll think no less of me for doing it.

Arrie, I certainly admire you for the way that you treated me yesterday and all previous times that I've been with you. I do not blame you for saying what you did to me. I wanted to see just how much you really cared for me. I won't tease you that way again. I do not and have not doubted your words but you can't tell me just what you can show me. As I told you, actions speak louder than words. I do not want to ever give you up and I shant unless I see that you want me too. I'm thinking now about some future day in next June when you and I shall be married. Everything that I am as can ever be is yours and yours only. I love you and you alone.

Answer soon, yours Sam

P.S. I've thought of the cuckee burs several times today.

November 10, 1919

Dearest,

I did not forget the milk when I got home this morning, I drank all that Mama had, almost a half gallon. Not very much but I made out with it.

Don't know whether I'll go to Georgia or not, if don't will call and see you Sunday afternoon.

Arrie, I wish that could see you right now. Suspect though that you would not get rid of me in time to sleep any tonight. I'd hate to make you lose two nights sleep in succession. But I'd really like to be with you, now. Yesterday I felt just like I was yours and I feel the same way now. Gee! But I like to feel that way. I'm perfectly natural when I feel that you care for me. It's only when I think of past days that I'm not natural. Please write real soon to you own true and affectionate, Sam

November 20, 1919
7:00 PM

Dearest,

Am feeling very well, I hope that you are feeling fine in every way. I wrote a letter to you Monday evening but Mama did not mail it on Tuesday and I did not care for it to go after then. So I tore it up. It was no fault of Mama's that she did not mail it. The mail man did not come by our house on Tuesday.

Arrie, if nothing hinders I'll be at your home on next Sunday afternoon. Did think that I'd not see you then but I just can't resist the temptation. I must see you then. Now, you told me to come to your home when I wanted to, if I came to often you have my permission to look like you did not want me that is if you do not want to tell me plainly. I'm never going to say any more about this now because I judge that you want me to visit you until I don't have to.

I've just been wondering why you tell me nothing about your school? You once told me all about it in your letters but now you do not even mention it when I'm with you. Is it possible that you have lost interest in teaching?

I hope that you can read this, I'm writing on my knee it's too cold to get away from the fire. I won't ask you to answer because I'll see you before you can. Yours, Sam Riggins

November 26, 1919
7:00 PM

My dearest,

In compliance with your request and because I want to, am letting you know by return mail that I received your letter today (Wednesday) and was more than delightful to get it.

Have been working today and feeling fine, better than dandy, I hope that you to have been well and happy.

Arrie, if I'm not sick and I don't suppose that I will be on next Sunday I'll call at your home in the afternoon to see you.

With lots of love and kisses, I am wishing a happy Thanksgiving tomorrow. Yours always, Sam Riggins

P. S. I have no paper except this.

February 17, 1920
7:30 PM

Dear Arrie,

I've purchased no paper yet but Mattie found this small piece and gave it to me. Am going to use it. I know that you had rather I would write just one sheet and stay by the fire than to go to the store for paper and write two. Now hadn't you?

I've been thinking of you since Sunday - in fact I'm always thinking of you. And I've thought too of both of our futures. I'm like you I like to think of the time when you and I will be together and will think together.

But now I'm willing for you to finish your school and I'll promise you that I'll be just as good and clean then as I am now. I will agree with you that it is hard to do, but you are worth it. I am willing to do the hardest things for you.

I will see you Sunday afternoon - in fact every Sunday afternoon until I tell you otherwise.

Yours, Sam

February 23, 1920
1:00 PM

Dear Arrie,

I would be real happy today had I not treated you as I did on last evening. Am so sorry that I did. Of course you have forgiven me but you cannot forget, can you? All that I can do is treat you the very best that I can from now on. I feel terribly bad about it. It seems to me that I try unintentionally to take advantage of good treatment for I know that you have never mistreated me in the least. I'll promise to do what ask me to last night, you remember I'm sure.

I am sending the pictures which were taken at your home two weeks ago, please let Nelle have hers. Only four were good. I had to stop work today at 9 o'clock on account of rain, maybe it will be fair tomorrow. I should try to write this letter over but I could do no better, am so nervous that I cannot write.

Will it be alright for me to visit you Sunday You may be tired of me. I could not blame you either. Yours always, Sam

March 22, 1920
7:40 PM

My dearest,

I've arrived back here today on train #12 but tarried for a short time only. I felt better when he brought the news that David's people were getting along fairly well. Mama did not come back today, I don't know when she's coming but I'm not worrying just at this time about her not being here.

Perhaps I'd better inform you that Papa went to Liberty to work else you might think David and family were still in a very bad condition. I hope that you had no difficulty getting to your school this morning. I've an idea that you got there all right because I know that you started on time.

You know everything that I do, therefore, I'll stop for now.

Your husband, Sam

END NOTES:

---

[i] This collection of letters is the personal collection of Dr. Ruth Looper of Hiawassee, Georgia, Professor of Literature at Young Harris College. Sam Riggins and Arabella Smith were her grandparents and she was most generous in allowing Rainbow Crow Publishing to edit the collection for our First World War Letter Collection Series.

[ii] *Ancestry.com*, "Samuel Leonard Riggins," ancestry.com/genealogy/records/Samuel-leonard-riggins-24-2xgmt9, accessed July 16, 2021.

[iii] *libertysc.com*, "City of Liberty: Start Here, Travel Here," libertysc.com/history, accessed July 19, 2021.

[iv] *theworldwar.org*, "Loaf of Bread: Baking During a Time of Crisis," November 24, 2020, theworldwar.org/learn/wwi/baking, accessed July 19, 2021. Ward Baking Company declared in 1920 that American Baking Industries flourished during the Great War. The federal reorganization of the food supplies served to change how Americans ate, prepared, and thought about food. Food scientists focused on bread making. Government commissioned studies on baking and milling to figure out the best ways to economize both the processes and utilizations of wheat during the war. It was determined that calories from bread amounted to approximately 30% of an individual's nourishment. In Sam's letters, there are many references to the troops receiving from those on the home front, cakes, cookies, sweets, and other types of baked items.

[v] *worldwar1centennial.org*, "American Aviation: The U.S. Army Air Service," worldwar1centennial.org/index.php/edu-home/edu-topics/591-birth-of-an-army-spring-1918/4999-american-aviation-the-u-s-army-air-service.html, accessed July 19, 2021. The U.S. Army had only 35 pilots when the American Expeditionary Force joined the allies in Europe. All planes and pilots were in the signal corps. The Aviation squadron entered combat in February 1918. One of America's most famous World War One Aces was the retired race car driver Eddie Rickenbacker.

[vi] This reference is the Furman University, which is a private liberal arts university in Greenville, South Carolina. It was founded in 1826 and became a secular university in 1992.

[vii] Pamela D. Toler, *time.com*, "Not Every Woman Who Served With the U.S. Military

During World War I Got the Same Treatment: Here's Why," February 26, 2019, time.com/5537784/wwi-us-military-women/time, accessed July 19, 2021. The role of women in the First World War varied according to the Military's needs. Many women signed up as ambulance drivers, telephone operators, munitions workers, and in Bolshevik Russia, there were all-female units. When America entered the war on April 6, 1917, two thousand women were enlisted as "Yeoman(f)" and when the Armistice was signed in 1919 there were approximately 11,000 women who had enlisted to fill the ranks in the army's regiments.

viii Haley Aaron, *worldwar1centennial.org*, "A Waltz and A Foxtrot: Dance Cards of World War I," April 18, 2018, worldwar1centennial.org/index.php/alabama-wwi-blog/4340-a-waltz-and-a-fox-trot-dance-cards-of-wwi.html, accessed July 19, 2021. Dances during the First World War were held for the benefit of soldiers away from home. Dance cards were used with the selection of songs and men would reserve the type of dance or tune with the ladies attending. The most popular dance steps were the Foxtrot and the Waltz.

ix Michael Harlon and Mike Iavarone, *worldwar1.org*, "Doughboy Center: The Story of the American Expeditionary Forces," last updated 2000, worldwar1.com/dbc/ymca.htm, accessed July 19, 2021. This section pertains to the history of the YMCA in the First World War. The YMCA was a conduit for services for the men in the military units. Historically, the Young Men's Christian Association helped armed forces with spiritual, mental, and physical strength by providing for their well-being and human needs. Typewriters, letter writing material, and pencils and pens were provided as parts of the services the YMCA provided as well as canteens for food and beverages such as coffee and water.

x *worldwar1centennial.org*, "Camp Forrest," last updated 2013, worldwar1centennial.org/index.php/component/gmapfp/394:camp-forrest.html?view=gmapfp, accessed July 19, 2021. Sam was most likely at Camp Forrest located northeast of Chattanooga around Tullahoma, Tennessee. Companioned with Camp McLean at Fort Oglethorpe, Georgia. Soldiers were housed in wooden barracks erected with monuments of confederate dead from the Battlefield of Chickamauga. These camps trained infantry engineers.

xi *nps.gov*, "Chickamauga Park," nps.gov/chch/learn/historyculture/index.htm, accessed July 19, 2021. In the summer of 1863, Confederate General Braxton Braff battled Union Troops under Union General William Rosecrans. The memorial site became Camp Forrest in the First World War.

xii Frederick Holmes, *kumc.edu*, "Venereal Disease," edited by the University of Kansas Medical Center, "Medicine in the First World War," July 28, 2018, kumc.edu/wwi/index-of-essays/venereal-disease.html, accessed July 19, 2021. President Wilson's religious affiliation assisted in providing programs to educate American Soldiers on European culture. 'Soldiers were ordered to be chaste.' Sam references his love for Arabella and reiterates that their relationship was very important to him. Therefore, he would abstain from sexual relationships. The military was instrumental in providing a campaign of lectures and posters to remind American Military men to be safe sexually.

xiii *Archives.lib.umn.edu*, "Trench and Camp," archives.lib.umn.edu/repositories/7/resources/882, accessed July 22, 2021. The Kautz Family YMCA archives in the Elmer L. Andersen Library at the University of Minnesota is a repository for many of the copies of the 'Trench and Camp' newsletters distributed to American Soldiers during the First World War. These were published by the YMCA's National War Work Council for various U.S. Army Camps. Contributions from Soldiers were included in the publications. These were many different perspectives of their experiences and remained as avenue of communication between the encampments between 1917-1919.

xiv Wilson A. Heefner, *worldwar1.com*, "Doughboy Center: The Story of the American Expeditionary Forces 'Machine Gun Battalion,'" worldwar1.com/dbc/divmguns.htm, accessed July 22, 2021. The machine gun units entered combat with the 1914 model of the French made Hotchkiss. These units served in both 'ground combat support and antiaircraft roles.'

xv *Chapmanculturalcenter.org*, "Spartanburg, SC," chapmanculturalcenter.org/pages/calendar/detail/event/a/e1829/, accessed July 22, 2021. *schistory.net*, "Tent and Trench, "edited by Jonathan Brooke and the Spartanburg County Historical Association, schistory.net/campwadsworth/, accessed July 22, 2021. From 1917 to 1919, Camp Wadsworth was one of America's premier army mobilization centers. Over 100,000 soldiers trained at the camp.

xvi Robert Hitchings, *pilotonline.com*, "Norfolk had a big voice in WWI," December 2, 2018, pilotonline.com/history/columns/article_7a9cf93e-e77a-11e8-91ae-e7658a4fd823.html, accessed July 22, 2021. Many famous singers entertained troops in camps and at the front. Besides Grace Kerns, who as known as the "Nightingale of the Trenches," there were many who came to sing for the men. Grace Kerns braved the war front and sang at the camps during the Battle of the Argonne. Another famous singer who was President Woodrow Wilson's daughter, Margaret Wilson, was most likely the one who Sam referenced in this letter as the "Miss Wilson" who sang at the Y #99. Margaret Wilson was educated at Goucher College in Baltimore and instructed in both voice and piano at the Peabody Institute of Music.

xvii J.W. Lawrance, *polkcounty.org*, "Landrum," April 15, 1998, polkcounty.org/county/landrum/landrum.html, accessed July 22, 2021. Landrum is a town next to Tryon, North Carolina. During the First World War, the soldiers at Camp Wadsworth would do artillery training near these towns on Hogback Mountain. One landmark in Landrum was its academy. This was a boarding high school but abandoned when the High School was moved to Grove, South Carolina before the First World War. Landrum's first high school graduates numbered six in the year 1916.

xviii Thomas E. Price, *6thinfantry.com*, "Sixth Division in France: 6th Infantry The Sightseeing 6th Infantry Division," 1996, 6thinfantry.com/about/a-brief-history-of-the-u-s-army-6th-infantry-division/, accessed July 22, 2021. The 6th infantry consisted of the 51st, 52nd, 53rd, and the 54th Infantry Regiments, along with the 16th, 17th, and 18th Machine Gun Battalions. The 3rd, 11th, and 78th Field Artillery Regiments were also part of the 6th Infantry. This group participated in the Argonne Offensive, patrolled "No Man's Land," and helped construct the trench system of the war. They returned to America June of 1919 aboard the USS Leviathan. The 6th Infantry was decommissioned at Camp Grant in Illinois on September 30, 1921.

xix *Airforcemag.com*, "Chronology: 1910-1919," November 24, 2018, airforcemag.com/chronology-1910-1919/, accessed July 22, 2021. On March 15, 1916, the first Aero Squadron organized and began its operations in the expedition against Mexico and Pancho Villa. By September of 1916, the first wireless radio was demonstrated in North Island, California. After many experiments, in February of 1917, the first voice was transmitted by wireless from an airplane to the ground in San Diego.

The Signal Corp reorganized in 1918 and became an official air corps of the war when President Woodrow Wilson signed and put into effect the Overman Act. The Aviation Section formed two agencies under the Secretary of war: (a) Bureau of Aircraft Production and (b) the Division of Military Aeronautics.

xx *Loc.gov*, "Stars and Stripes: The American Soldiers' Newspaper of World War I: 1918-1919," loc.gov/collections/stars-and-stripes/articles-and-essays/behind-the-scenes/military-censorship/, accessed July 22, 2021. The Army's Board of Control and its General Headquarters examined content of all articles. Most writing of journalists during the First World War needed to support the war effort by censoring its content. The aim of the military was to make sure the mission of the newspaper maintained high morale. Soldiers mail was many times censored by a commanding officer for words that might give away positions of the troops or relay sensitive information. Some letters that are in Special Collections at museums will often have black marker over certain phrases or parts of the letter cut away.

xxi Please see the entry for "Katydids" at Britannica.org/animal/long-horned-grasshopper

xxii Please visit the Arizona University Special Collections "The American Vaudeville Museum Archive" for examples of shows the soldiers would have seen. Speccoll.library.arizona.edu/collections/vaudeville/subject/world-war-i/

xxiii *history.com*, "Spanish Flu 1918," history.com/topics/world-war-i/1918-flu-pandemic, accessed July 23, 2021. The Spanish Flu pandemic of 1918 was at that point in history the deadliest in history. An estimated 500 million people worldwide were infected. Between 20 and 50 million lives were lost. One unusual aspect of the 1918 flu was that it had attacked healthy, young people including many WWI servicemen. President Woodrow Wilson contracted the flu in 1919 while negotiating the Treaty of Versailles.

xxiv Pascal Trequer, *wordhistories.net*, "Cooties and Lice in the Trenches," wordhistories.net/2018/01/03/cootie-wwi-orgin/, accessed July 23, 2021. Cootie is a noun and a slang term for "body louse." It was first noted in 1917 on the Western Front in the trenches.

xxv "Old Bob" is a horse.

xxvi *Knowitall.org*, "Overhere: The Homefront during WWI," knowitall.org/video/over-here-homefront-during-wwi-part-1-anti-war, accessed July 23, 2021. In 1917, South Carolina was more rural than urban. People lived in areas with cotton fields and still relied on horses and buggies for transportation. Industry, particularly the textiles flourished in the Carolinas. Picking cotton was part of this industry's process for making textiles.

xxvii This reference to "Mr. Wilson" is a reference to President Woodrow Wilson.

xxviii *nps.gov*, "Private Albert Cooper and the 318th Engineers at Vancouver Barracks," nps.gov/articles/albertcoopervancouverbarracks.htm, accessed July 23, 2021. The birthplace of the 318th Engineers was on the banks of the Columbia River by Portland, Oregon. The 318th Engineers in the First World War were responsible for building pontoon bridges and digging trenches. The 318th embarked for the front from Camp Merritt, New Jersey by several different ships: *SS American* and *SS Washington* and from New York on the *SS Dekalb.* Once in Brest, France the 318th built warehouses, barracks, and water supply systems along with laying railroad systems.

xxix Gloucester, South Carolina is an area around Hilton Head.

xxx Lt. Colonel Edwin L. Kennedy, ausa.org, "Mass-producing Leaders: WWI Army

Needed a Lot of Officers – Quickly," June 19, 2017, https://www.ausa.org/articles/mass-producing-leaders-wwi, accessed July 23, 2021. Men who were leaders were needed for the war. Noncommissioned officers took years to develop. Usually in a group of eight one soldier was selected to be a corporal. Many candidates learned by doing, others went through schools or trainings in the camp. Noncommissioned officers were not similar to commissioned officers who are usually a Lieutenant or of higher ranking in the military.

xxxi *thecrimson.com*, "Beaune University," thecrimson.com/articles/1919/5/23/the-lesson-of-beaune-university-ptwenty/, accessed July 23, 2021. Beaune University is an American University twenty miles south of Dijon, France. This university was constructed by and for the American Expeditionary Forces to help educate their soldiers. 10,000 students had access to 200 study courses and could work towards a degree.

xxxii *history.amedd.army.mil*, "Office of Medical History, Base Hospital No. 120," history.amedd.army.mil/booksdoc/wwi/adminamerexp/chapter24.html, accessed July 23, 2021. The Base Hospital No. 120 was organized at Camp Greenleaf, Georgia on August 28, 1910. The Hospital Regiment embarked November 12, 1918, on the *Empress of Russia* for Brest, France. Base Hospital No. 120 operated at Kerhouon until January 10, 1919. After this date transferred to Tours and remained at Joue-Les-Tours until June 10, 1919. The command to demobilize (once back in the state) took place at Camp Dodge, Iowa, July 16, 1919.

xxxiii *Veteran-voices.com*, "Camp Jackson," veteran-voices.com/world-war-i-training-camps/camp-jackson/, accessed July 23, 2021. Camp Jackson was established in July 1917 as the training camp for the new 81st "Wildcat" Infantry Division of the National Army. From 1918 to 1919 the camp was engaged to act as a field artillery replacement depot and training center.

xxxiv *history.state.gov*, "The League of Nations, 1920," history.state.gov/milestones/1914-1920/league, accessed July 26, 2021. The League of Nations was an international organization headquartered in Geneva, Switzerland. It was created during the First World War as a forum for resolving disputes. The United States never joined even though President Woodrow Wilson was instrumental in constructing a foundation for its philosophy.

xxxv Doina Anca Cretu, *encyclopedia.1914-1918-online.net*, "Diphtheria," encyclopedia.1914-1918-online.net/article/health_disease_mortality_demographic_effects, accessed July 26, 2021. Lice and typhus were only several epidemics soldiers and civilians dealt with as the war started to unfold in 1914. Diphtheria, a childhood disease at that time, doubled in the war years. The disease symptoms ranged from a sore throat to the inability to breathe due to a 'false membrane' covering the larynx.

xxxvi *redcross.org*, "World War I and the American Red Cross," redcross.org/content/dam/redcross/National/history-wwi.pdf, accessed July 26, 2021. The Red Cross provided "huts" for soldiers as part of camp services. The Red Cross Huts supplied items such as clothing, comfort items, organized recreational activities, and provided welfare services such as nurses to write letters for servicemen unable to do so for themselves. They also provided, along with the YMCA, entertainment such as movies and refreshments.

xxxvii John Rieken, *georgiaencyclopedia.org*, "Fort McPherson," December 9, 2003, Last updated July 16, 2018, georgiaencyclopedia.org/articles/government-politics/fort-mcpherson, accessed July 26, 2021. Fort McPherson is located southwest of Atlanta. It encompassed approximately 500 acres. The fort was used primarily for "German military and merchant seamen interned" during the war. It was home to the General Hospital #6.

[xxxviii] For information about Lake Conestee, South Carolina, visit lakeconesteenaturepark.com or conesteepreserve.org.

[xxxix] Hymnology.hymnsam.co.uk, "Ruebush Kieffer Company," https:/www.hymnology.hymnsam.co.uk/r/ruebush-kieffer-company-usa, accessed July 26, 2021. In 1872, the Ruebush-Kieffer Company incorporated at Singer Glen, Virginia. The company was a Mennonite hymnal production company, and they compiled and printed a successful product titled *Harmonia Sacra.*

Bibliography:

Aaron, Haley. "A Waltz and A Foxtrot: Dance Cards of World War I." *The United States World War One Centennial Commission.* April 18, 2018. worldwar1centennial.org/index.php/alabama-wwi-blog/4340-a-waltz-and-a-fox-trot-dance-cards-of-wwi.html (accessed July 19, 2021).

"American Aviation: The U.S. Army Air Service." *The United States World War One Centennial Commission.* n.d. worldwar1centennial.org/index.php/edu-home/edu-topics/591-birth-of-an-army-spring-1918/4999-american-aviation-th-u-s-army-air-service.html (accessed July 19, 2021).

"Beaune University." *thecrimson.com.* n.d. thecrimson.com/article/1919/5/23/the-lesson-of-beaune-university-ptwenty/ (accessed July 23, 2021).

"Camp Forrest." *The United States World War One Centennial Commission.* 2013. worldwar1centennial.org/index.php/component/gmapfp/394:camp-forrest.html?view=gmapfp (accessed July 19, 2021).

"Camp Jackson." *Veteran Voices Military Research.* n.d. veteran-voices.com/world-war-i-training-camps/camp-jackson/ (accessed July 23, 2021).

"Chronology: 1910-1919." *Air Force Magazine.* November 24, 2018.

airforcemag.com/chronology-1910-1919/ (accessed July 22, 2021).

"City of Liberty: Start Here, Travel Here." *libertysc.com.* n.d. libertysc.com/history (accessed July 19, 2019).

Cretu, Doina Anca. "Health, Disease, Mortality; Demographic Effects ." *1914-1918 Online International Encyclopedia of the First World War.* n.d. encyclopedia.1914-1918-online.net/article/health_disease_mortality_demographics_effects (accessed July 23, 2021).

Frederick Holmes, MD. "Medicine in the First World War 'Venereal Disease'." *University of Kansas Medical Center.* July 26, 2018. kumc.edu/wwi/index-of-essays/venereal-disease.html (accessed July 19, 2021).

Heefner, Wilson A. "Doughboy Center: The Story of the American Expeditionary Forces 'Machine Gun Battalion'." *worldwar1.com.* n.d. worldwar1.com/dbc/divmguns.htm (accessed July 22, 2021).

"History and Culture 'Chickamauga Park'." *National Park Service.* n.d. nps.gov/chch/learn/historyculture/index.htm (accessed July 19, 2021).

Hitchings, Robert. "Norfolk had a big voice in WWI." *pilotonline.com.* December 2, 2018. pilotonline.com/history/columns/article_7a9cf93e_e77a_11e8_91ae_e7658a4fd823.html (accessed July 22, 2021).

Iavarone, Michael Harlon and Mike. "Doughboy Center: The Story of the American Expeditionary Forces." *worldwar1.com.* 2000. worldwar1.com/dba/ymca.htm (accessed July 19, 2021).

Kennedy, Lt. Colonel Edwin L. "Mass-producing Leaders: WWI Army Needed a Lot of Officers-Quickly." *Association of the United States Army.* June 19, 2017. https://www.ausa.org/articles/mass-producing-leaders-wwi (accessed July 23, 2021).

Lawrance, J. W. "Landrum." *polkcounty.org.* April 15, 1998. polkcounty.org/county/landrum/landrum.html (accessed July 22, 2021).

"Loaf of Bread: Baking During a Time of Crisis." *National WWI Museum and Memorial.* November 24, 2020. theworldwar.org/learn/wwi/baking/ (accessed July 19, 2021).

"Office of Medical History: Base Hospital No. 120." *history.amedd.army.mil.* n.d. history.amedd.army.mil/booksdocs/wwi/adminamerexp/chapter24.html (accessed July 23, 2021).

"Overhere: The Homefront during WWI." *knowitall.org.* n.d. knowitall.org/video/over-here-homefront-during-wwi-part-1-anti-war (accessed July 23, 2021).

Price, Thomas E. "Sixth Division in France: 6th Infantry The Sightseeing 6th Infantry Division." *6thinfantry.com.* 1996. 6thinfantry.com/about/a-brief-history-of-the-u-s-army-6th-infantry-division/ (accessed July 22, 2021).

"Private Albert Cooper and the 318th Engineers at Vancouver Barracks." *National Park Service.* n.d. nps.gov/articles/albertcoopervancouverbarracks.htm (accessed July 23, 2021).

Rieken, John. "Fort McPherson." *New Georgia Encyclopedia.* December 9, 2003. georgiaencyclopedia.org/articles/government-politics/fort-mcpherson (accessed July 26, 2021).

"Samuel Leonard Riggins." *ancestry.com.* n.d. ancestry.com/genealogy/records/samuel-leonard-riggins-24-2xgmt9 (accessed July 16, 2021).

"Spanish Flu 1918." *history.com.* n.d. history.com/topics/world-war-i/1918-flu-pandemic (accessed July 22, 2021).

"Spartanburg, SC." *chapmanculturalcenter.org.* August 17, 2017. chapmanculturalcenter.org/pages/calendar/detail/event/a/e1829/ (accessed July 22, 2021).

"Stars and Stripes: The American Soldiers' Newspaper of World War I: 1918-1919." *Library of Congress.* n.d. loc.gov/collections/stars-and-stripes/articles-and-essays/behind-the-scenes/military-censorship/ (accessed July 22, 2021).

Brooke, Jonathan, ed. "Tent and Trench." *South Carolina History.* n.d. schistory.net/campwadsworth/ (accessed July 22, 2021).

"The League of Nations, 1920." *Office of the Historian.* n.d. history.state.gov/milestones/1914-1920/league (accessed July 26, 2021).

"Trench and Camp." *archives.lib.umn.edu.* n.d. archives.lib.umn.edu/repositories/7/resources/882 (accessed July 22, 2021).

Trequer, Pascal. "Cooties and Lice in the Trenches." *wordhistories.net.* n.d. wordhistories.net/2018/01/03/cootie-wwi-orgin/ (accessed July 23, 2021).

"World War I and the American Red Cross." *redcross.org.* n.d. redcross.org/content/dam/redcross/National/history-wwi.pdf (accessed July 26, 2021).

www.ingramcontent.com/pod-product-compliance
Ingram Content Group UK Ltd.
Pitfield, Milton Keynes, MK11 3LW, UK
UKHW041642190726
13854UKWH00006B/2652